SCREAM GEMS

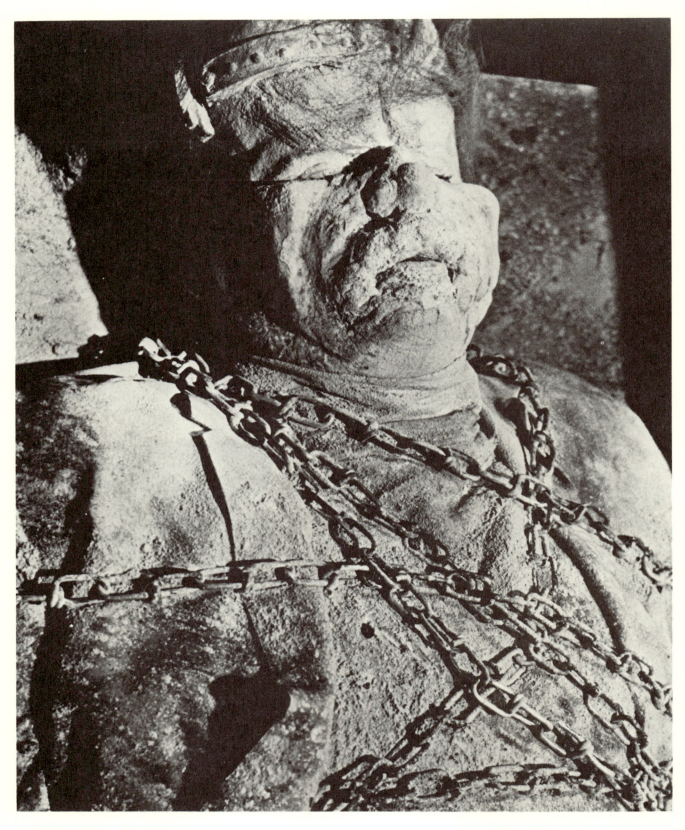

"Dracula vs. Frankenstein"
starring J. Carrol Naish · Lon Chaney · Regina Carrol
with Zandor Vorkov as "Dracula"

SCREAM GEMS

GEMS

MARK BARAKET

DRAKE PUBLISHERS INC. NEW YORK•LONDON

ACKNOWLEDGMENTS

The author is grateful to the following individuals and organizations for helping to create *Scream Gems:*
Julie Palacios, American International Pictures Corp, Toho, Bryanston Distributors, Inc., Howard Mahler Films, Inc., Janus Films, Cannon Group, Inc., NMD Film Distributing Comp., Hemisphere Pictures, Inc., Graffitti Productions, Cambist Films, Inc., New Line Cinema Corp., Andy Warhol Enterprises, Inc., Amicus Prod. Ltd., Peppercorn Wormser Film Enterprises, Allied Artists Pictures Corp., Joseph Brenner Associates, Inc., Movie Star News, and Walter T. Baker. Film stills are copyrighted by the production and/or distribution companies.

Published in 1977 by
Drake Publishers Inc.
801 Second Avenue
New York, N.Y. 10017

Scream Gems
LC: 76-43414

ISBN: 0-8473-1466-9

Illustrations by Ted Enik

Printed in the United States of America

CONTENTS

Dedicated to both my wife Margarita,

whose understanding matches her loveliness,

and to my daughter Tamara

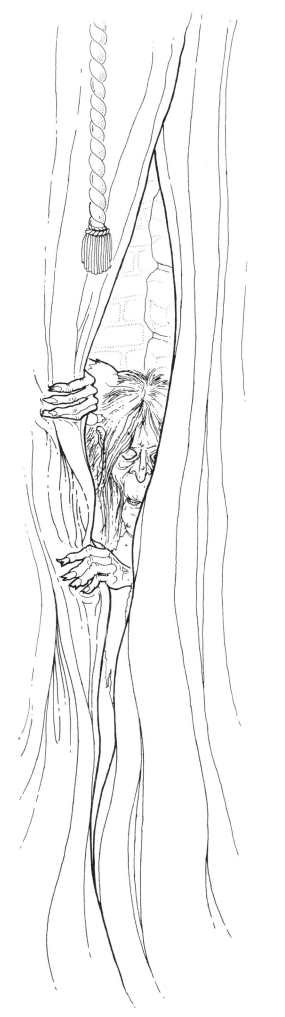

SCREAM GEMS

Scene from "Devil's Nightmare"

INTRODUCTION

VAMPIRES, UNDYING MONSTERS, giant-sized monsters, alien beings! Which of us hasn't been frightened by cinema's myriad monster machine at one time or another? The horror film has touched all of us, either as children, teens, or adults and is the oldest form of cinematic art. Each passing year brings a new form to the cinema of horror. Kids of the thirties and forties were scared out of their wits by such distinguished gentlemen of horror as Lugosi, Chaney, Karloff, and Atwill: the fifties turned a new generation onto teenage werewolves, giant-sized monsters, insects, and things from the Black Lagoon. Horror cinema has no specific definition: what scares one person may not necessarily scare another; what some consider horror, others do not. Perhaps the only thing that does differentiate it from other forms of cinema is its appeal to young and old alike in screenplays vivid with fantastic imagery removed from everyday life and not based on established fact.

I have assembled my favorite horror, science-fiction, and fantasy films and have further divided the genres into specific classes to compare horror, science-fiction, and fantasy films with each other. The book is unique in that major motion pictures are described in the text, while most of the stills are from rare and contemporary films and are not found in similar works on the subject. If I have offended anyone by omitting favorite stills or films, I am sorry. I have included films that many fans, buffs, and collectors may not be aware of. I hope that you will find the book both entertaining and unusual— I have tried to make it so.

chapter 1

NOCTURNAL CREATURES

HORROR IS DEFINED by the dictionary as intense fear, pain, dread, aversion, or repugnance. This description is perhaps the best way to explain the screen's oldest form of cinematic art. What is horror? Is it the dark mansion that affords protection from thunder and lightning? Is it the infusion of eternal life into something dead, the mystery behind the wrappings of a 5000-year-old antiquity? Is it the apparition of a fiendish beast or the insight into the mind of a psychopathic killer? Although the horror film encompasses all of these bizarre images, it is basically escapist entertainment. Its popularity has never ceased to wane throughout cinema history because of the escape from reality that it offers. All of us have at one time or another loved the feeling of being frightened out of our wits while we are safe in the confines of our divans or movie seats.

The horror film drew its inspiration from the field of literature. A prolific group of writers showed the diverse areas of horror. Wells inspired the field of science fiction, as did Jules Verne. Stoker, Stevenson, Shelley, and Poe gave horror a reputation of distinction and desirability. Of the many types of horror the oldest must surely be the vampire. The role of the vampire in literature began in 1847 with the appearance of *Varney the Vampire, or Feast of Blood*. Lord Byron himself wrote a vampire story. Joseph Sheridan LeFanu's *Carmilla,* one of the best vampire stories in print, also served as a blueprint for an opera, *Carmen*. By 1897 the best-known literary vampire was *Dracula,* written by Bram Stoker. But literature isn't the only source of horror-oriented tales. Mystery stage plays also

13

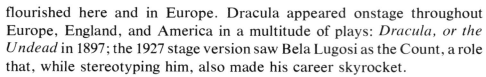

flourished here and in Europe. Dracula appeared onstage throughout Europe, England, and America in a multitude of plays: *Dracula, or the Undead* in 1897; the 1927 stage version saw Bela Lugosi as the Count, a role that, while stereotyping him, also made his career skyrocket.

Among the few lesser-known vampire films are VAMPIRE'S TRAIL (1910), DANSE VAMPIRESQUE (1912), and A VILLAGE VAMPIRE (1916). The first true adaptation of the classic *Dracula*, NOSFERATU, was made in Germany in 1922 by F.W. Murnau. The film is a takeoff on the Stoker classic, and, to prevent infringement on the copyright, screenwriter Henrik Galeen changed the setting, the characters' names, and the physical makeup of the main character.

Murnau's tale is alive with many outdoor settings, a different style from the Universal production based on the 1927 stage play. Hutter (Gustav Von Wangenheim) is a realtor sent to the Carpathians to procure a piece of land for a Count Orlock. The film infuses fantasy with Hutter's vision of reality, as in Orlock's appearance as the driver of a black-shrouded coach driven at an unnatural pace. Galeen's Orlock is the most horrible of the screen character portrayals, quite different in style from the description of a well-mannered gentleman in Stoker. Orlock is hideous, with an egg-shaped head, bushy eyebrows, a broken, longish nose, and pointy ears. Murnau's NOSFERATU changes locale when Orlock boards a ship that pulls into the port of Bremen. It is a ghost ship: the entire crew is dead and a multitude of rats pour out, implying a plague. Hutter's wife Ellen knows better and sacrifices herself by staying with him until the rays of dawn cause him to vanish!

1927's LONDON AFTER MIDNIGHT cast Lon Chaney as Police Inspector Burke, a vampire killer. Universal's 1931 production cast Bela Lugosi as the Count, a repetition of his stage role. Tod Browning's direction and Garrett Ford's screenplay are shown in the detailed miniatures of Dracula's castle and Carfax Abbey and in Lugosi's portrayal of the well-mannered European gentleman. A Spanish version was also filmed at the same time, with Carlos Villarias as Count Dracula. Carl Dreyer's VAMPYR, a 1932 French film, was adapted from LeFanu's *Carmilla*. Blood drinking is implied more than shown.

The vampire continued to proliferate in films such as VAMPIRE BAT

"The Living Coffin", a rarely seen Mexican film

(1932), CONDEMNED TO LIVE (1935), and MGM's MARK OF THE VAMPIRE, a 1935 remake of *London After Midnight* with Bela Lugosi and Carol Borland. Lugosi played Count Mora. Universal's sequel, DRACULA'S DAUGHTER, was made in 1936 by Carl Laemmle. The film begins where Dracula left off, with Edward Van Sloan's Van Helsing put on trial for two murders after police find him with the bodies of Dracula and Renfield. Gloria Holden is cast as Countess Maria Zaleska, who journeys to London to claim the body of her fanged father. She is under his influence and herself obsessed with blood drinking, again implied rather than shown. The film is also noted for the first scene of a female vampire attacking another female. This bit of horror would later become more perverse and shocking, but here the attack is made off-camera and depicted by shadows against a wall.

Lugosi continued his vampire roles in the 1940 films VAMPIRE BAT and SPOOKS RUN WILD. SON OF DRACULA (1943) cast Lon Chaney, Jr. in the Universal production directed by Bob Siodmak. Chaney was cast as Count Alucard (Dracula spelled backwards) after the inhabitants of the Caldwell plantation from *Dark Oaks*. RETURN OF THE VAMPIRE (1943) was followed by THE VAMPIRE'S GHOST (1945) from Republic, RKO'S ISLE OF THE DEAD, DEVIL BAT'S DAUGHTER (1946), and OLD MOTHER REILLY MEETS THE VAMPIRE (1952). United Artist's THE VAMPIRE depicts a doctor who turned into a vampire. Violence slightly increased when Cousin Bellac (Francis Lederer) was impaled on a stake in a pit after having amorous designs on one of his family members in UA's CURSE OF DRACULA (1958).

American International's BLOOD OF DRACULA (1957) cast Sandra Harrison as a pretty student under the influence of a college hypnotist who turned her into a bushy-eyebrowed, fanged female. By this time interest in the area was waning. The genre of the vampire film was becoming more and more anemic in its attempts to scare the viewer. It got the transfusion it needed from a British donor, Hammer studios.

HORROR OF DRACULA (1958) starred Christopher Lee, a handsome gentleman cultured in the art of seduction. Produced by Michael Carrerras, directed by Terence Fischer, and written by Jimmy Sangster, the film marks the turning point in established horror or what will shock. Lee brings to the surface his obsession with blood, mixed with sexual domination and lust. The character as well as the story comes closer to Stoker's classic than

A scene from "Vampire People", a Philippine-made horror film

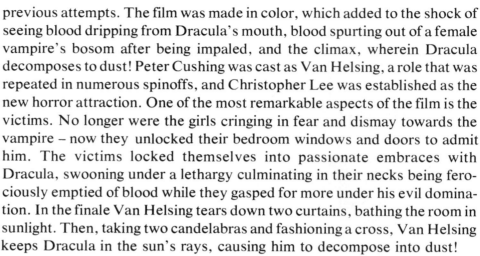

previous attempts. The film was made in color, which added to the shock of seeing blood dripping from Dracula's mouth, blood spurting out of a female vampire's bosom after being impaled, and the climax, wherein Dracula decomposes to dust! Peter Cushing was cast as Van Helsing, a role that was repeated in numerous spinoffs, and Christopher Lee was established as the new horror attraction. One of the most remarkable aspects of the film is the victims. No longer were the girls cringing in fear and dismay towards the vampire – now they unlocked their bedroom windows and doors to admit him. The victims locked themselves into passionate embraces with Dracula, swooning under a lethargy culminating in their necks being ferociously emptied of blood while they gasped for more under his evil domination. In the finale Van Helsing tears down two curtains, bathing the room in sunlight. Then, taking two candelabras and fashioning a cross, Van Helsing keeps Dracula in the sun's rays, causing him to decompose into dust!

BLOOD OF THE VAMPIRE (1958) was about a doctor, Callistrautus, while CURSE OF THE UNDEAD (1959) was set in the West and featured a gunslinging vampire outlaw. From Italy came I VAMPIRI (1957), while Mexico gave us German Robles as Count Lavud in EL VAMPIRO and EL ATUD DEL VAMPIRO (both 1959). Hammer's BRIDES OF DRACULA (1960) featured David Peel as Baron Meinster, while in Don Sharp's KISS OF THE VAMPIRE (1963) a honeymoon couple fell prey to vampires. The film culminates in the bride bared naked before a coven of vampires and initiated into a cult, the first implication of nudity, which was on the increase in similar horror films.

Barbara Steele appeared in numerous Italian horror films, among them LA DANZA MACABRE (1963), in which she surfaced as a lesbian vampire, and GLI AMANTI D OLTRE TOMBA, where she was chained to a wall and whipped. On the lighter side, UNCLE WAS A VAMPIRE (1959) cast Christopher Lee as a vampire who fed himself on scantily clad hotel guests. Mario Bava's excellent BLACK SABBATH (1963) was a trilogy of tales that evoked gloom and evil by its use of black-and-white photography and gothic settings: *A Drop Of Water* is a Chekov story about raising the dead; *The Telephone* is about a murderer who plagues a pretty girl over the telephone; a story by Tolstoy headlines the trilogy, *The Vurdalak*. Boris Karloff is cast as a family patriarch who is slowly becoming a vampire living off his relations.

Italy also spurred the rise of another horror star, Walter Brandi. Brandi

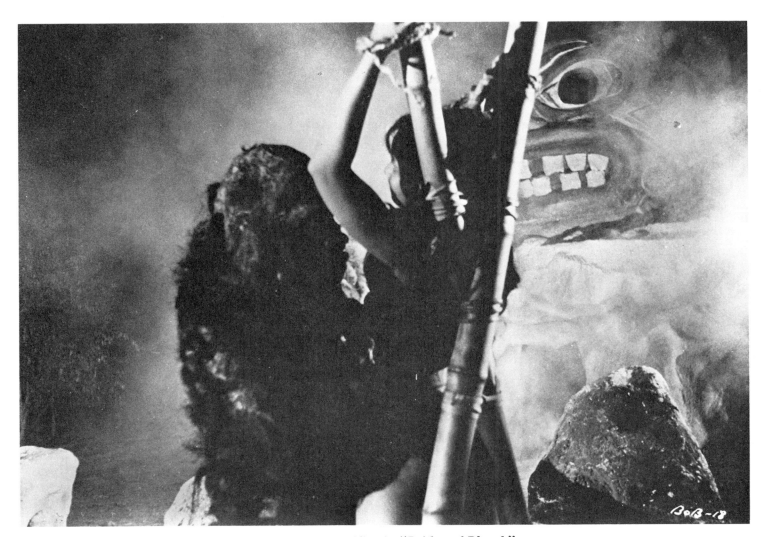

Human sacrifice in "Brides of Blood"

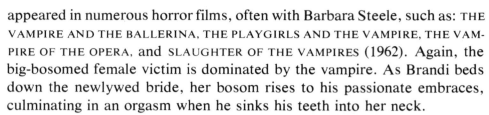

appeared in numerous horror films, often with Barbara Steele, such as: THE VAMPIRE AND THE BALLERINA, THE PLAYGIRLS AND THE VAMPIRE, THE VAMPIRE OF THE OPERA, and SLAUGHTER OF THE VAMPIRES (1962). Again, the big-bosomed female victim is dominated by the vampire. As Brandi beds down the newlywed bride, her bosom rises to his passionate embraces, culminating in an orgasm when he sinks his teeth into her neck.

Roger Vadim's BLOOD AND ROSES (1960) was the first serious attempt to bring LeFanu's *Carmilla* to the screen. The film opens at Castle Karnstein, where a neice, Mircalla, is slowly coming under the spell of vampirism through the rotting corpse of her relative Carmilla, which is kept in part of the castle. Mircalla soon turns to blood drinking and lusts after Leopoldo, the fiancé of her rival Georgia. Leopoldo represents another relative, Ludwig, whom Carmilla loved. In a dream sequence Carmilla as Mircalla dreams that she has attacked Georgia, hoping to become her and claim Leopoldo's affections. Leopoldo marries Carmilla, not Georgia, unbeknownst to him. Vadim's film hints heavily at lesbianism in scenes between Elsa Martinelli and Annette Vadim. Claude Renoir's photography is rich and blends well with Vadim's direction.

Mexico combined vampires with masked wrestlers in a number of horror films. Vampires continued a source of horror in many Mexican efforts, such as: THE BODY SNATCHER (1956), CURSE OF NOSTRADAMUS, BLOOD OF NOSTRADAMUS, GENII OF DARKNESS, and THE MONSTER DEMOLISHER. Santo, a wrestler hero, fought vampires in REVENGE OF THE VAMPIRE WOMEN. In EL MUNDO DE LOS VAMPIROS the vampires sing their National Anthem during drives for recruits!

Despite many foreign vampire films, Christopher Lee continued to be synonymous with the character. Hammer added many spinoffs to HORROR OF DRACULA with Peter Cushing's Van Helsing character. DRACULA, PRINCE OF DARKNESS (1966), DRACULA HAS RISEN FROM THE GRAVE (1968), TASTE THE BLOOD OF DRACULA, SCARS OF DRACULA (1970), DRACULA (1972), COUNT DRACULA (1970), and SATANIC RITES OF DRACULA (1973) all followed, each film growing in violence, gore, and sex. Other vampires surfaced in DEVILS OF DARKNESS (1965) and THEATER OF DEATH (1966), wherein Christopher Lee was the owner of a grand-guignol-type theater where murders occurred. American International's BLOOD BATH (or TRACK OF THE VAMPIRE)

"Curse of the Vampires" with Amelia Fuentes sleeping in her coffin

featured William Campbell as a hippie artist who axed pretty models and placed their corpses in vats of boiling wax. FEARLESS VAMPIRE KILLERS, or PARDON ME BUT YOUR TEETH ARE IN MY NECK (1967), was a satire by Roman Polanski featuring his wife Sharon Tate as Sarah, who is abducted from her bath by a Count Krolock. BLOOD OF DRACULA'S CASTLE (1969), MALENKA (1969), BLOOD BEAST TERROR, BLOOD DEMON (1968), and VALERIE AND HER WEEK OF WONDERS (1969) added to the list of vampire films. ISLE OF THE DEAD (1966), VAMPIRE PEOPLE, BLOOD DRINKERS, and BRIDES OF BLOOD (1969) were horror shockers from the Philippines, while Mexico offered SANTO AND THE BLUE DEMON VS THE MONSTERS (1968) and SANTO AND THE TREASURE OF DRACULA. Japan's contributions were LAKE OF DRACULA (1972) and VAMPIRE DOLL.

Hammer elaborated on LeFanu's *Carmilla* with a trilogy of lesbian-oriented vampire tales. THE VAMPIRE LOVERS (1970) cast Ingrid Pitt as Mircalla Karnstein in a Roy Ward Baker film. Mircalla seems fascinated by the bosoms of her victims prior to blood drinking. Jimmy Sangster's sequel was LUST FOR A VAMPIRE (1971), starring Utte Stensgard as Mircalla, who claims her victims at a finishing school. Lesbianism, tremendous outpourings of blood, and throat slashing, with a pretty girl providing the lifeblood for Mircalla's corpse, immerses the viewer in shock upon shock. TWINS OF EVIL ended the Karnstein trio of horror, with Peter Cushing cast as a witch hunter. Lesbianism continued to flourish in COUNTESS DRACULA (1971), with Ingrid Pitt cast as Countess Elizabeth Bathory, a real-life countess who thought virgin blood made her skin look younger. Another film based on the real-life exploits of the Countess stars Paloma Picasso, New Line Cinema's IMMORAL TALES (1975). VAMPIRE CIRCUS (1972) was another Hammer film, while Mike Raven returned as Count Karnstein in DISCIPLE OF DEATH (1973). Lesbianism flourished in other vampire tales, such as: HANNAH QUEEN OF VAMPIRES, which infused sadism into the sexual domination of the vampire over the victim. Jean Rollin's vampire films revel in rapes, eye gouging, torture, sadism and lesbianism.

CURSE OF THE VAMPIRES, a 1970 Hemisphere film, showed vampirism as an obsession in the breakdown of an entire family. Eduardo, the vampire-obsessed brother, claims his beautiful sister as his victim. Eduardo's blood drinking is the culmination of sexual domination and rape. After he tells a

*Count Dracula (Udo Keir) recovers after discovering that his latest victim
(Stefanie Cassini) is not a virgin*

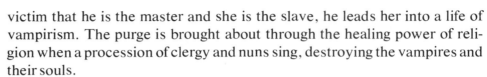

victim that he is the master and she is the slave, he leads her into a life of vampirism. The purge is brought about through the healing power of religion when a procession of clergy and nuns sing, destroying the vampires and their souls.

American made horror films were also turning to the vampire as a continued area of fright fare and box-office cash. American International dominated the area with such films as DEATHMASTER, with Robert Quarry as a guru vampire who enslaves a commune of youths into a life of vampirism. In the climax a girl is drained of blood by an entire cult of vampires. Quarry was previously cast as COUNT YORGA (1970) and RETURN OF COUNT YORGA (1971), while William Marshall was a black vampire in AIP's BLACULA and the 1973 sequel SCREAM, BLACULA, SCREAM. THE BAT PEOPLE upset a Midwest town, while CAPTAIN KRONOS VAMPIRE HUNTER (1973), was unleashed on a horror double bill. Kung Fu, a short-lived fad, was featured in THE LEGEND OF THE SEVEN GOLDEN VAMPIRES (1974), starring Peter Cushing. David Niven became OLD DRACULA, also with Teresa Graves as a black vampirina, while Dan Curtis' famed soaper *Dark Shadows* materialized on celluloid as HOUSE OF DARK SHADOWS, with Jonathan Frid again playing the role of Barnabas Collins. GRAVE OF THE VAMPIRE (1973) told of a son who vows vengeance on his vampire father. Andy Warhol, so successful with his Frankenstein 3-D, cast Udo Keir as ANDY WARHOL'S DRACULA (1975), another parody on old-time horror-film monsters brought up to date with explicit sex and gore.

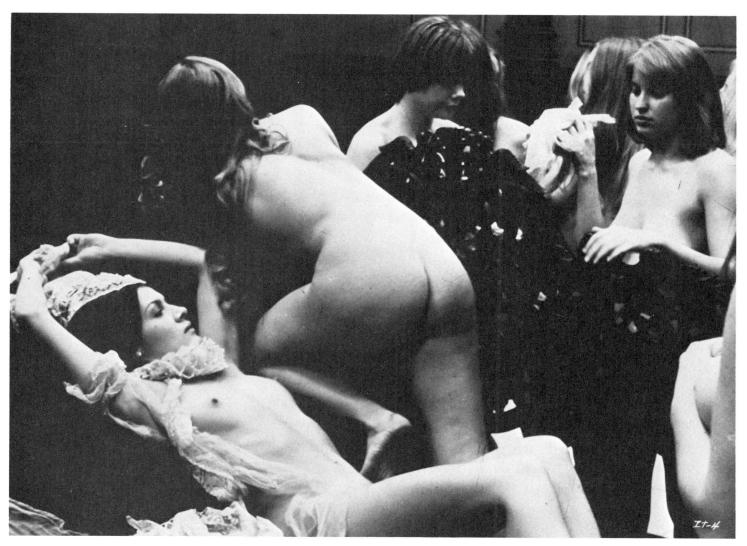

Sex has become a big part of the vampire-oriented film

chapter 2

AND MAN-MADE

MARY WOLLSTONECRAFT SHELLEY, her husband Percy Bysshe Shelley, and Lord Byron were living in Geneva in 1816. Since it rained frequently, the group was confined indoors. To pass the time, all wrote a story. Soon teenage Mary had finished a Gothic novel, published in 1817 as *Frankenstein*. It told the tale of a man's efforts to emulate God and create life. The creation lives, turns on his creator, and wreaks havoc until he is destroyed, along with his maker. This tale serves as the basis for a number of horror films. Thomas Alva Edison's film company made a short one-reeler of the novel in 1910. Charles Ogle played the monster. He looked nothing like his contemporaries but was in fact closer to Mary Shelley's description, created with a number of chemicals rather than electricity.

The best-known version is the 1931 Universal classic FRANKENSTEIN, starring Boris Karloff as the monster and Colin Clive as his creator, Henry. James Whale's direction is excellent, infusing the right amount of black humor into the dialogue and using sets such as the graveyard and burning-windmill sequences to convey atmospheric terror. The film was also provided with a gimmick. Edward Van Sloan, who is in the film, emerges on-stage before the credits to warn the audience that the tale is not for the weak of heart and people that faint easily. Censorship periled the film in the creation scene, where Henry, ecstatic about his creation's moments of life, shouts:"It's alive! It's alive! At last I know what it feels like to be God!" That bit of dialogue was snipped, along with a scene where a little girl, Maria, is tossed into a pond by the monster to see if she floats. All we are left

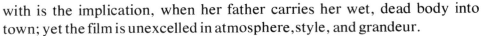

with is the implication, when her father carries her wet, dead body into town; yet the film is unexcelled in atmosphere, style, and grandeur.

In the 1935 sequel BRIDE OF FRANKENSTEIN Whale surpassed himself with even more black humor and religious imagery, as in the mock crucifixtion of the monster by the villagers and the mock marriage of monster to monster in the climax. The film's gimmick lies in Mary Shelley relating her tale to her husband and Lord Byron prior to the actual story. Her words melt into the ruins of the windmill, and the action takes up where the original left off. Elsa Lanchester is the bride, seated at the monster's side. The monster pats her hand, causing her to emit a reptilian snarl. The monster goes berserk, shouting, "She hate me like others!" Before destroying the castle he manages to tell his creator, "Go! We belong dead!" Frank Waxman's musical score fits the action beautifully. Interestingly enough, the same score was also used in FLASH GORDON.

Further sequels were mere parodies of the originals, never again emulating the style of the classics. Whale left his job as a director, and his style went with him. Along with Karloff, he was able to evoke pathos from the audience, who saw the monster as a mute, frightened child. Gone was the symbolism of the monster's first glimpse of the world. As a roof is rolled back, a dungeon is suddenly bathed in light, causing the monster to look up and grasp for the light, similar to a child emerging from the womb. The sequels showed the monster as a murderous brute as evidenced in SON OF FRANKENSTEIN (1939) and GHOST OF FRANKENSTEIN (1942). Universal combined monsters for profit's sake in FRANKENSTEIN MEETS THE WOLFMAN (1943). The monster continued to flourish in such films as Universal's HOUSE OF FRANKENSTEIN and HOUSE OF DRACULA (1944) and retired in ABBOTT COSTELLO MEET FRANKENSTEIN (1948) with Bela Lugosi, Lon Chaney, Jr., and Lenore Aubert.

Hanmer studios infused the monster with British blood in a number of films starring Peter Cushing as the Baron. CURSE OF FRANKENSTEIN (1957) offered Cushing as the Baron and Christopher Lee as the creation. Director Terence Fischer and screenwriter Jimmy Sangster combined talents to give viewers gore, dismembered limbs, innocent sex, and, in some cases, interesting allegory. On the other hand, silly, low-budget films using the name proliferated in the late fifties: I WAS A TEENAGE FRANKENSTEIN (1957), HOW TO MAKE A MONSTER (1958), both from AIP, FRANKENSTEIN (1970), from

Karloff plays the Baron in "Frankenstein 1970", Allied Artists'
contribution to the genre

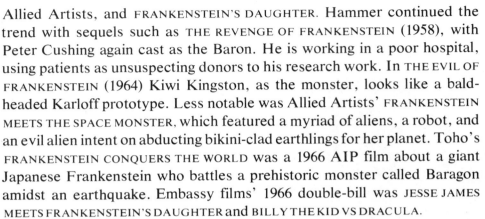

Allied Artists, and FRANKENSTEIN'S DAUGHTER. Hammer continued the trend with sequels such as THE REVENGE OF FRANKENSTEIN (1958), with Peter Cushing again cast as the Baron. He is working in a poor hospital, using patients as unsuspecting donors to his research work. In THE EVIL OF FRANKENSTEIN (1964) Kiwi Kingston, as the monster, looks like a bald-headed Karloff prototype. Less notable was Allied Artists' FRANKENSTEIN MEETS THE SPACE MONSTER, which featured a myriad of aliens, a robot, and an evil alien intent on abducting bikini-clad earthlings for her planet. Toho's FRANKENSTEIN CONQUERS THE WORLD was a 1966 AIP film about a giant Japanese Frankenstein who battles a prehistoric monster called Baragon amidst an earthquake. Embassy films' 1966 double-bill was JESSE JAMES MEETS FRANKENSTEIN'S DAUGHTER and BILLY THE KID VS DRACULA.

Hammer's FRANKENSTEIN CREATED WOMAN (1967) again offered Peter Cushing as the Baron in a Terence Fischer film. The soul of a woman's lover, who was framed for murder, is placed into her lovely body after she has committed suicide. She enacts revenge on the framers, after which she again chooses to commit suicide. Christina (Susan Denberg) is depicted as a hermaphroditic murderess, seducing her victims prior to the kill. Cushing, on the other hand, is cast as a supermaker, providing us with the first soul transplant. Fischer has given the film a mythological, imaginative, almost allegorical style, preferring not to go the route of cheap, sensationalistic porn. Fischer's last film in the series was FRANKENSTEIN MUST BE DESTROYED (1969). Here the Baron has infused his creation with his colleague's brain, giving it life. Freddie Jones portrays the pathetic creature, who goes berserk after discovering that his newly acquired body and soul turns off his wife. HORROR OF FRANKENSTEIN (1970) was directed by Jimmy Sangster, who cast Ralph Bates as the Baron, a creator devoid of any sort of humanity, as opposed to Cushing's Baron. The film was interspersed with a fair amount of sexuality and violence. FRANKENSTEIN AND THE MONSTER FROM HELL (1973) brought back Peter Cushing as the Baron. The creation is a hairy, apelike creature rather than the usual prototype.

A flood of Frankenstein horror films appeared in the early seventies, never matching the quality of Universal or Hammer. FRANKENSTEIN ON CAMPUS was about a student being thrown out of a college for possessing drugs and going off to create a monster. Independent International made a trilogy of Frankenstein horror films, starting with DRACULA VS

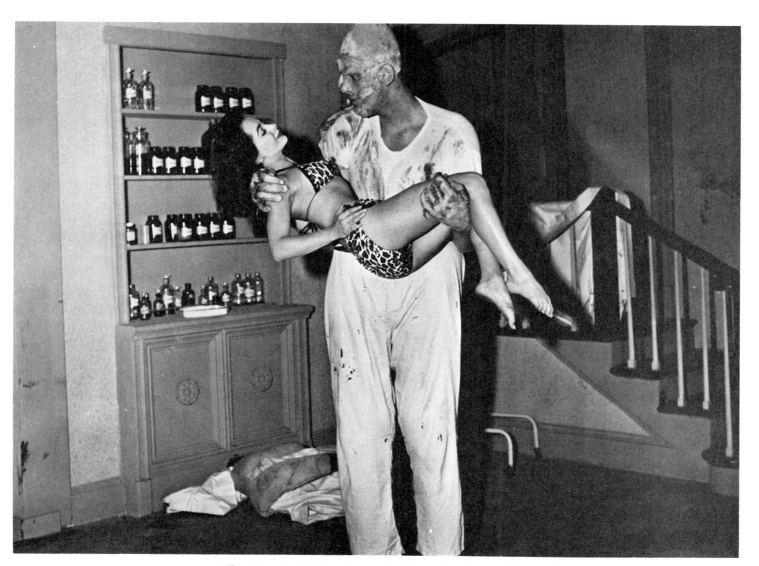

Allied Artists' "Frankenstein Meets the Space Monster"

FRANKENSTEIN (1971). The film features the two monsters abducting big-bosomed blondes and operating out of an amusement-park horror house. FRANKENSTEIN'S BLOODY TERROR featured Paul Naschy as a werewolf but no Frankenstein. BLOOD OF FRANKENSTEIN (1972) also emphasized big-bosomed blondes. BLACKENSTEIN, LADY FRANKENSTEIN, MUNSTER GO HOME, and Mel Brook's YOUNG FRANKENSTEIN (1975) all added to the genre. The latter was a parody of the first three Universal films and was also done in "glorious black-and-white."

ANDY WARHOL'S FRANKENSTEIN 3-D (1975) was more visually interest-ing, offering the gimmick of three dimensional glasses. Viewers could see dismembered limbs, fornication on a female zombie's gall bladder, and innards ripping out of torsos and pouring into the lap, all in glorious gore and 3-D! The process, while not perfect, isn't bad. It takes only a few minutes to get used to the stereoscopic glasses. The process is shot in a one-camera technique called spacevision, that utilizes a special prism to cast two images of the same object at different angles. Bryanston's film combines 3-D, incest, nudity, sex, necrophilia, and gore in a true cult film, one that provides an interesting approach to a tired subject. EMBRYO (1976) takes an adult approach to the age-old story. Rock Hudson has created a beautiful girl, played by Barbara Carreras. She matures into a beautiful woman in a short time. He falls in love with her, resulting in the downfall of the man and his creation in an interesting tale.

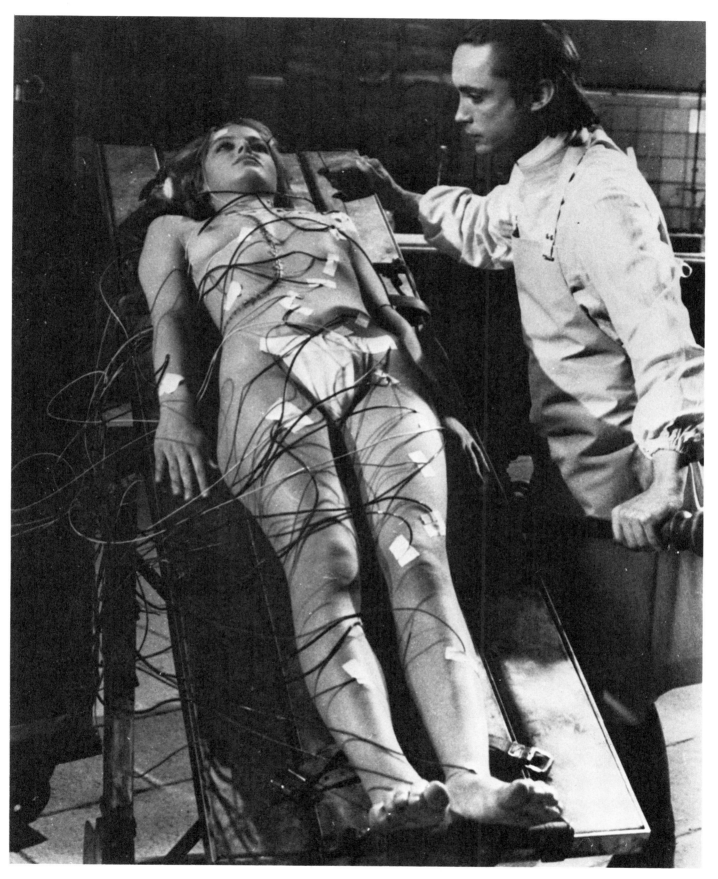

*The Baron (Udo Keir) admires his newly created girl zombie in
Andy Warhol's "Frankenstein" 3-D*

Willis O'Brien's "The Lost World"

chapter 3

CELLULOID HORRORS

HORROR FILMS HAVE INDEED emerged as a main staple for film buffs to feast
on. Whetting their appetites on such delicacies as DRACULA, FRANKENSTEIN,
KING KONG, THE EXORCIST, and JAWS, each year brings a new twist to the
genre of film horror. Why they are not just a short-lived fad, as the spy-hero
or kung-fu-killer crazes, to name a few, still remains a mystery. They offer
mass appeal in numerous ways. By appealing to various age groups they
give all of us that thrill of being frightened out of our wits. Children
encounter dragons, ogres, and witches in numerous fairytale adaptations on
celluloid. The teenage audience thrills to blood-curdling terror tales about
fiendish killers and psychos, while the adult viewer may be equally ab-
sorbed in a classic old-house thriller from the golden age when each mystery
had to feature a haunted house with sliding doors and the mysterious
cloaked red herring. Cinema's crude beginnings in the area of screen horror
came from literature. H.G. Wells inspired the science-fiction thriller, while
Poe gave much to the Gothic horror film.

George Melies, the father of fantasy, gave us the screen's first imaginative monster in his 1912 production THE CONQUEST OF THE POLE, wherein a
polar expedition meets up with a hungry abominable snowman. MIDNIGHT
EPISODE (1899) featured the screen's first giant insect, while MAGIC SWORD
(1901) offered the first giant. Apes were used as a source of horror in

35

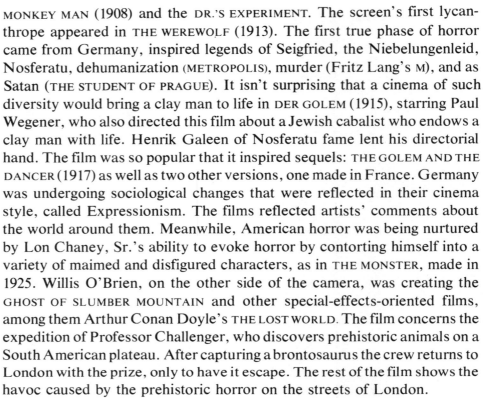

MONKEY MAN (1908) and the DR.'S EXPERIMENT. The screen's first lycanthrope appeared in THE WEREWOLF (1913). The first true phase of horror came from Germany, inspired legends of Seigfried, the Niebelungenleid, Nosferatu, dehumanization (METROPOLIS), murder (Fritz Lang's M), and as Satan (THE STUDENT OF PRAGUE). It isn't surprising that a cinema of such diversity would bring a clay man to life in DER GOLEM (1915), starring Paul Wegener, who also directed this film about a Jewish cabalist who endows a clay man with life. Henrik Galeen of Nosferatu fame lent his directorial hand. The film was so popular that it inspired sequels: THE GOLEM AND THE DANCER (1917) as well as two other versions, one made in France. Germany was undergoing sociological changes that were reflected in their cinema style, called Expressionism. The films reflected artists' comments about the world around them. Meanwhile, American horror was being nurtured by Lon Chaney, Sr.'s ability to evoke horror by contorting himself into a variety of maimed and disfigured characters, as in THE MONSTER, made in 1925. Willis O'Brien, on the other side of the camera, was creating the GHOST OF SLUMBER MOUNTAIN and other special-effects-oriented films, among them Arthur Conan Doyle's THE LOST WORLD. The film concerns the expedition of Professor Challenger, who discovers prehistoric animals on a South American plateau. After capturing a brontosaurus the crew returns to London with the prize, only to have it escape. The rest of the film shows the havoc caused by the prehistoric horror on the streets of London.

The 1920s saw the emergence of the old-house thriller as a source of horror. This phase of horror is concerned with scenarios built around deserted mansions and haunted houses, complete with sliding panels, creaky doors, and shadows cast on walls lit by candlelight. THIRTEENTH HOUR (1927) starred Lionel Barrymore. One of the best of this type was THE CAT AND THE CANARY (1927), directed by Paul Leni. LAST WARNING (1928) and CHAMBER OF HORRORS (1929) followed. THE TERROR (1928), directed by Roy Del Ruth, was adapted from an Edgar Wallace thriller. Chaney gave his all in a multitalented role in THE UNHOLY THREE (1930). Like EXCITING NIGHT (1922), THE BAT (1926) was a play developed for the screen. It was directed by Roland West from the Mary Reinhart and Avery Hopwood play. The sequel, THE BAT WHISPERS, was made in 1931. Another mystery film using an eerie setting was Rupert Julien's THE CAT CREEPS, the sequel to CAT AND THE CANARY. Based on John Willard's story, the film was later remade as a comedy vehicle for Bob Hope.

"The Aztec Mummy", a Mexican film

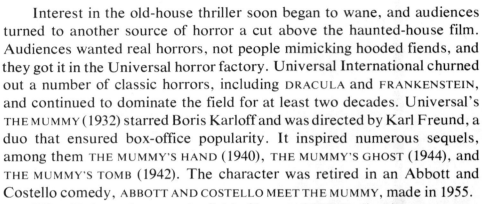

Interest in the old-house thriller soon began to wane, and audiences turned to another source of horror a cut above the haunted-house film. Audiences wanted real horrors, not people mimicking hooded fiends, and they got it in the Universal horror factory. Universal International churned out a number of classic horrors, including DRACULA and FRANKENSTEIN, and continued to dominate the field for at least two decades. Universal's THE MUMMY (1932) starred Boris Karloff and was directed by Karl Freund, a duo that ensured box-office popularity. It inspired numerous sequels, among them THE MUMMY'S HAND (1940), THE MUMMY'S GHOST (1944), and THE MUMMY'S TOMB (1942). The character was retired in an Abbott and Costello comedy, ABBOTT AND COSTELLO MEET THE MUMMY, made in 1955.

What Universal was to the field of horror RKO Radio Pictures was to adventure films. In 1932 Merian C. Cooper and Ernest B. Schoedsak combined their resources to create one of the most famous variations on the Beauty and the Beast tale ever made, KING KONG. Max Steiner's musical score amplifies the special effects of Willis O'Brien with its cast of Robert Armstrong, Bruce Cabot, and Fay Wray, the film continues to be as popular now as it was then. Through the magic of stop-motion animation O'Brien created Kong and the magnificent dense, tropical jungle sequences with deep mattes and glass shots. SON OF KONG (1933) brought back Robert Armstrong with Helen Mack and a white ape equally as terrifying as his father.

WEREWOLF OF LONDON (1935) starred Henry Hull as the lycanthrope in a story written for Universal by Robert Harris. The Ritz Brothers were menaced by THE GORILLA in 1939. Paramount's THE MONSTER AND THE GIRL featured George Zucco as a red herring, while Lionel Atwill was a maniac who infused Lon Chaney, Jr., with electric life in MAN-MADE MONSTER (1941). Universal further dominated the horror field by adding a new character, THE WOLFMAN (1941), with Lon Chaney, Jr., as Larry Talbot, who at a full moon turns into a ravaging wolf, slaying victims until his father, played by Claude Rains, kills his son in a typical Universal setting—a mist-shrouded marshland—as he is just about to claim another victim, played by Evelyn Ankers. Based on a Curt Siodmak screenplay, the character is enlivened by Jack Pierce's masterful makeup.

The monster is radioactive as well as awesome in "The Giant Behemoth"

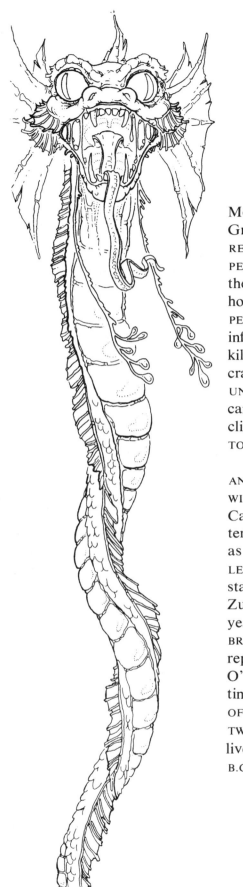

INVISIBLE WOMAN (1941) followed, as did INVISIBLE AGENT (1942). Monogram studios, a maker of grade B fright films, cast Karloff as Dr. Grath in THE APE, which inspired APEMAN (1943) with Bela Lugosi and RETURN OF THE APEMAN (1944). RKO'S CAT PEOPLE and CURSE OF THE CAT PEOPLE, made two years later, were screen examples of implied horror from the mind of Val Lewton. The implication in the viewers' mind provoked the horror. Working on this principle, he hired Jacques Tourneur to direct CAT PEOPLE. The film tells the story of a girl who believes that she is under the influence of a curse and that, when aroused sexually, will turn into a feline killer. Irena (Simone Simon) dies in the climax after being wounded and crawling towards a zoo to rest with her friends. Twentieth Century Fox's UNDYING MONSTER (1942) was a werewolf. The next phase of film horror came out of the serials of the forties, the Saturday-afternoon action-oriented cliffhangers that ended with the words "To be continued" (See MAD DOCTORS, MAD SCIENTISTS, AND HEAVIES).

Other forties fiends included MONSTER MAKER (1944), Republic's LADY AND THE MONSTER, made the same year, and Universal's trilogy, CAPTIVE WILD WOMAN (1943), JUNGLE WOMAN, and JUNGLE CAPTIVE (1945). John Carradine was usually the mad doctor, while lovely girls were the feline terrors—Aquannetta, for one. Females continued to provide horror, such as Nina Foch in Columbia's CRY OF THE WEREWOLF. HAIRY APE and LEOPARD MAN followed in 1944. Paramount's MAN IN HALF MOON STREET stayed alive with organ transplants from unwilling donors, while George Zucco was back as another red herring in FLYING SERPENT (1946). In that year Republic's CATMAN OF PARIS menaced Lenore Aubert. Universal's BRUTE MAN was Rondo Hatton, a real acromegalic-faced horror. Hatton repeated his role in THE CREEPER (1948) and HOUSE OF HORRORS. Willis O'Brien was back with apes in MIGHTY JOE YOUNG (1949). Gorillas continued as a source of horror in Columbia's MARK OF THE GORILLA and BRIDE OF THE GORILLA. UNCHARTED ISLAND featured prehistoric monsters, as did TWO LOST WORLDS. The special effects amounted to no more than the use of live lizards combined with distance shots of cast members in ONE MILLION B.C. (1940), which starred Victor Mature and Carol Landis.

In 1953 there was a change in film horror in addition to the demise of the

"How to Make a Monster" combines the teenage werewolf and the teenage Frankenstein from previous films

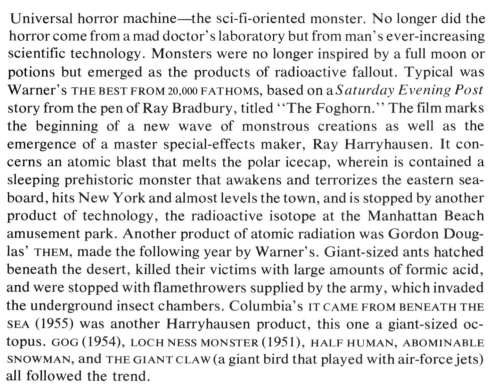

Universal horror machine—the sci-fi-oriented monster. No longer did the horror come from a mad doctor's laboratory but from man's ever-increasing scientific technology. Monsters were no longer inspired by a full moon or potions but emerged as the products of radioactive fallout. Typical was Warner's THE BEST FROM 20,000 FATHOMS, based on a *Saturday Evening Post* story from the pen of Ray Bradbury, titled "The Foghorn." The film marks the beginning of a new wave of monstrous creations as well as the emergence of a master special-effects maker, Ray Harryhausen. It concerns an atomic blast that melts the polar icecap, wherein is contained a sleeping prehistoric monster that awakens and terrorizes the eastern seaboard, hits New York and almost levels the town, and is stopped by another product of technology, the radioactive isotope at the Manhattan Beach amusement park. Another product of atomic radiation was Gordon Douglas' THEM, made the following year by Warner's. Giant-sized ants hatched beneath the desert, killed their victims with large amounts of formic acid, and were stopped with flamethrowers supplied by the army, which invaded the underground insect chambers. Columbia's IT CAME FROM BENEATH THE SEA (1955) was another Harryhausen product, this one a giant-sized octopus. GOG (1954), LOCH NESS MONSTER (1951), HALF HUMAN, ABOMINABLE SNOWMAN, and THE GIANT CLAW (a giant bird that played with air-force jets) all followed the trend.

THE DEADLY MANTIS (1957) was Universal's contribution to the atomic-mutation-products list. The mantis played with the air-force, only to be gassed beneath the Holland tunnel. Warner's THE BLACK SCORPION menaced Mexican officials and helicopters. United Artists' THE MONSTER THAT CHALLENGED THE WORLD (1957) was a sac that produced a radioactive mutant—a caterpillar with fangs—which was destroyed with a fire extinguisher! Allied Artists' THE GIANT BEHEMOTH (1959) was another giant radioactive prehistoric monster that menaced Londoners by burning their skin with a horrible radiation. It was destroyed by a radioactive torpedo! Some down-to-earth-sized terrors were AIP's I WAS A TEENAGE FRANKENSTEIN with Gary Conway and I WAS A TEENAGE WEREWOLF with Michael Landon, who turned into a wolf at the sound of the school bell. Universal's last great creature was THE CREATURE FROM THE BLACK LAGOON

Caltiki devours his latest victim in Allied Artists'
"Caltiki, the Immortal Monster"

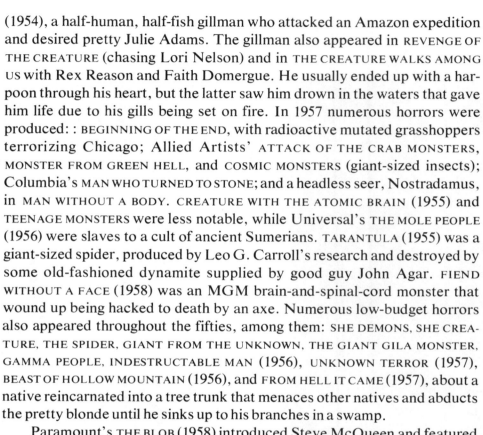

(1954), a half-human, half-fish gillman who attacked an Amazon expedition and desired pretty Julie Adams. The gillman also appeared in REVENGE OF THE CREATURE (chasing Lori Nelson) and in THE CREATURE WALKS AMONG US with Rex Reason and Faith Domergue. He usually ended up with a harpoon through his heart, but the latter saw him drown in the waters that gave him life due to his gills being set on fire. In 1957 numerous horrors were produced: : BEGINNING OF THE END, with radioactive mutated grasshoppers terrorizing Chicago; Allied Artists' ATTACK OF THE CRAB MONSTERS, MONSTER FROM GREEN HELL, and COSMIC MONSTERS (giant-sized insects); Columbia's MAN WHO TURNED TO STONE; and a headless seer, Nostradamus, in MAN WITHOUT A BODY. CREATURE WITH THE ATOMIC BRAIN (1955) and TEENAGE MONSTERS were less notable, while Universal's THE MOLE PEOPLE (1956) were slaves to a cult of ancient Sumerians. TARANTULA (1955) was a giant-sized spider, produced by Leo G. Carroll's research and destroyed by some old-fashioned dynamite supplied by good guy John Agar. FIEND WITHOUT A FACE (1958) was an MGM brain-and-spinal-cord monster that wound up being hacked to death by an axe. Numerous low-budget horrors also appeared throughout the fifties, among them: SHE DEMONS, SHE CREATURE, THE SPIDER, GIANT FROM THE UNKNOWN, THE GIANT GILA MONSTER, GAMMA PEOPLE, INDESTRUCTABLE MAN (1956), UNKNOWN TERROR (1957), BEAST OF HOLLOW MOUNTAIN (1956), and FROM HELL IT CAME (1957), about a native reincarnated into a tree trunk that menaces other natives and abducts the pretty blonde until he sinks up to his branches in a swamp.

Paramount's THE BLOB (1958) introduced Steve McQueen and featured a giant-sized blob of ooze that fed itself on people, growing and growing until it is stopped with fire extinguishers. Similar blobs of matter were Allied's CALTIKI THE IMMORTAL MONSTER (1959) and BEWARE THE BLOB (1972). Fox studio's contribution was THE FLY (1958), which inspired RETURN OF THE FLY (1959) and CURSE OF THE FLY (1965). The fifties' low-budget style of film horror was advertised in poster campaigns that often promised more than they delivered. Typical was a poster for THE WASP WOMAN, which featured a giant wasp ensnaring a victim but materialized on celluloid as Gloria Talbot sporting a wasp head and a set of claws, the product of beauty treatments involving wasp enzymes. Similar makeup jobs

"King Kong vs Godzilla" was made with two endings: in the Japanese version Godzilla wins, while King Kong is the winner in the American version

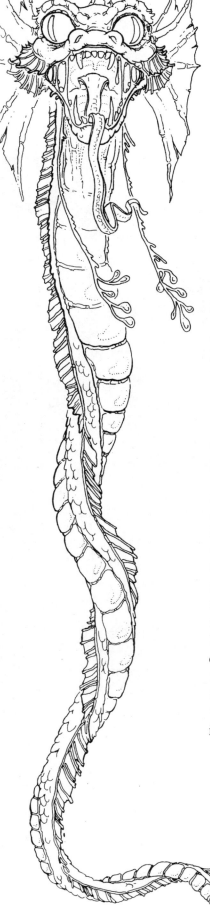

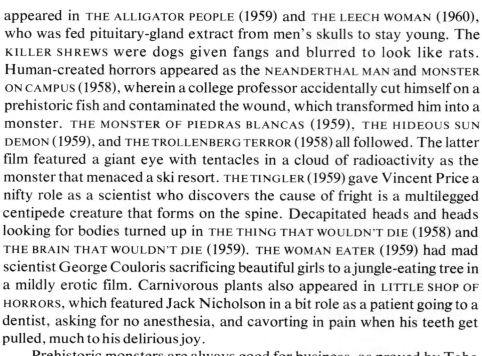

appeared in THE ALLIGATOR PEOPLE (1959) and THE LEECH WOMAN (1960), who was fed pituitary-gland extract from men's skulls to stay young. The KILLER SHREWS were dogs given fangs and blurred to look like rats. Human-created horrors appeared as the NEANDERTHAL MAN and MONSTER ON CAMPUS (1958), wherein a college professor accidentally cut himself on a prehistoric fish and contaminated the wound, which transformed him into a monster. THE MONSTER OF PIEDRAS BLANCAS (1959), THE HIDEOUS SUN DEMON (1959), and THE TROLLENBERG TERROR (1958) all followed. The latter film featured a giant eye with tentacles in a cloud of radioactivity as the monster that menaced a ski resort. THE TINGLER (1959) gave Vincent Price a nifty role as a scientist who discovers the cause of fright is a multilegged centipede creature that forms on the spine. Decapitated heads and heads looking for bodies turned up in THE THING THAT WOULDN'T DIE (1958) and THE BRAIN THAT WOULDN'T DIE (1959). THE WOMAN EATER (1959) had mad scientist George Couloris sacrificing beautiful girls to a jungle-eating tree in a mildly erotic film. Carnivorous plants also appeared in LITTLE SHOP OF HORRORS, which featured Jack Nicholson in a bit role as a patient going to a dentist, asking for no anesthesia, and cavorting in pain when his teeth get pulled, much to his delirious joy.

Prehistoric monsters are always good for business, as proved by Toho Productions, Ltd. GODZILLA (1956), with special effects by Eiji Tsuburuya, spurred a flood of similar Toho films, in some of which Godzilla changed into a national hero and battles with other monsters ready to do in Japan. GIGANTIS THE FIRE MONSTER (1959) attacked Japan, while MGM's GORGO (1961) went looking for its offspring throughout London. AIP's KONGA (1960) was a giant ape that attacked London, the product of heavy Michael Gough's scientific experiments. Toho continued to import monsters of all shapes and sizes. MOTHRA (1962) was a giant moth turned caterpillar turned butterfly. RODAN was a flying monster that devoured giant insects before destroying Japan. Other Nipponese imports were; GORATH, GAPPA, VARAN, THE MANSTER, DAGORA, YANGORA, GAMMERA (1965), a giant turtle, GHIDRAH, THREE-HEADED MONSTER (1964), ATROGAN, MAJIN (1966), GYAAS, VIRAS, JIGER, and others. Toho also mixed monsters in an equally entertaining number of films, the first of which was KING KONG VS GODZILLA (1963).

Godzilla and Mothra in "Ghidrah, Three-Headed Monster"

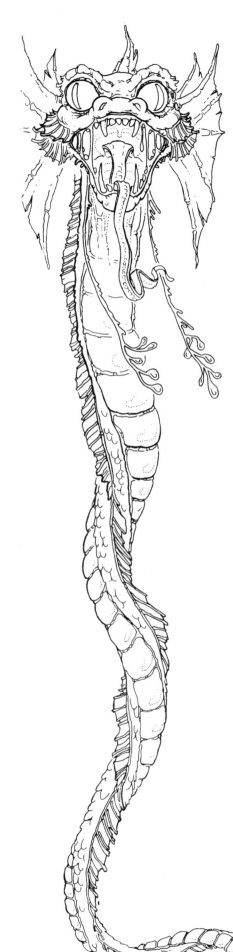

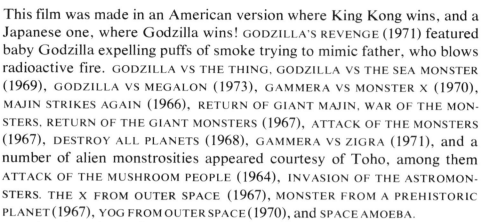

This film was made in an American version where King Kong wins, and a Japanese one, where Godzilla wins! GODZILLA'S REVENGE (1971) featured baby Godzilla expelling puffs of smoke trying to mimic father, who blows radioactive fire. GODZILLA VS THE THING, GODZILLA VS THE SEA MONSTER (1969), GODZILLA VS MEGALON (1973), GAMMERA VS MONSTER X (1970), MAJIN STRIKES AGAIN (1966), RETURN OF GIANT MAJIN, WAR OF THE MONSTERS, RETURN OF THE GIANT MONSTERS (1967), ATTACK OF THE MONSTERS (1967), DESTROY ALL PLANETS (1968), GAMMERA VS ZIGRA (1971), and a number of alien monstrosities appeared courtesy of Toho, among them ATTACK OF THE MUSHROOM PEOPLE (1964), INVASION OF THE ASTROMONSTERS. THE X FROM OUTER SPACE (1967), MONSTER FROM A PREHISTORIC PLANET (1967), YOG FROM OUTER SPACE (1970), and SPACE AMOEBA.

Another change in domestic horror was introduced by Hammer film studios of England, who made it big by redoing Universal monsters in color with gore, a little innocent sex, and better stories and settings. Typical remakes were THE MUMMY (1959) with Christopher Lee, which inspired two sequels, CURSE OF THE MUMMY'S TOMB (1964), and THE MUMMY'S SHROUD (1966). CURSE OF THE WEREWOLF (1961) featured Oliver Reed as Leon, a werewolf, the product of a savage rape of a mute servant girl by a maniacal caged beggar. Leon is born on Christmas Day and, when baptized, causes a fountain of holy water to boil. The priest sees this as an omen and informs Leon's father that the boy will become a ravenous beast when sexually provoked. The omen comes true when Leon slays a harlot at a bordello. Meanwhile, Bill Castle was setting himself up as a producer of gimmick-laden horror films—MR SARDONICUS (1961) helped him rake in big profits. CURSE OF THE FACELESS MAN (1958) searched for his lady love to the chagrin of good guy Richard Anderson. AIP's REPTILICUS was a giant serpent that attacked Copenhagen. THE SLIME PEOPLE, HORRORS OF SPIDER ISLAND, and American International's X—THE MAN WITH THE X-RAY EYES followed. A number of Mexican imports also surfaced: SAMSON IN THE WAX MUSEUM (1963), ADVENTURE AT THE CENTER OF THE EARTH, GOMAR, CURSE OF THE DOLL PEOPLE, VENGEANCE OF SEX, SANTO VS FRANKENSTEIN'S DAUGHTER (1966), CHABELITO AND PEPITO VS THE MONSTERS (1971), and a tag-teamed wrestler horror film, SANTO AND THE BLUE DEMON VS THE MONSTERS (vam-

"Man and the Monster", a Mexican film

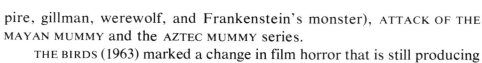

pire, gillman, werewolf, and Frankenstein's monster), ATTACK OF THE MAYAN MUMMY and the AZTEC MUMMY series.

THE BIRDS (1963) marked a change in film horror that is still producing offshoots. The film shows what can happen when nature and man goes out of sync and birds attack civilized people. Teleworld's THE FLESH EATERS (1964) were parasites that ate flesh. In one sequence a victim is drinking from a glass filled with the parasites, and the camera turns to a look of unbelieveable horror as he realizes that his stomach is coming out! Other films that take off on the idea were WILLARD (rats), BEN (more rats), AIP's FROGS (1972), THE DEADLY BEES, THE KILLER SNAKES, NIGHT OF THE LEPUS (giant rabbits), GIANT SPIDER INVASION (1975), and AIP's THE FOOD OF THE GODS (based on an H.G. Wells story about nature gone mad, with ravenous rats and other animals attacking humanity). JAWS (a man-eating shark), a 1975 Universal film based on the best seller by Peter Benchley, and GRIZZLY, a 1976 film about a rampaging bear with a preference for sexy campers, are recent variations.

WEREWOLF IN A GIRLS' DORMITORY (1961) infused lycanthorpy with soft-core porn. Del Tenny's HORROR OF PARTY BEACH (1964) involved radioactive mutants formed from waste material dumped in the ocean. The contorted gill creatures gorged themselves on the blood of beautifully endowed females. Sex emerged in horror films, as evidenced by BEACH GIRLS AND THE MONSTER (1965) and THE BEAST THAT KILLED WOMEN. In THE CREATURE'S REVENGE females were chained to dungeon walls while being drained of blood; rape is also implied. THE GORGON (1965) was a Hammer film about a Medusan; THE VULTURE and THE REPTILE (1966) followed. IT! (1967) was a stone statue brought to life by a madman. Japan continued to assault itself with the wrath of GODZILLA VS THE SMOG MONSTER and WAR OF THE GARGANTUAS. HORROR OF MALFORMED MEN (1969), SPIDER BABY (1968), and SOUND OF HORROR (1966) were above-average shockers. Warner's TROG (1970) was a neanderthal relic found in a cave by Joan Crawford, while Burt Reynolds met up with "Tropies" in SKULLDUGGERY (1970). Hemisphere Pictures was laden with horror from THE MAD DOCTOR OF BLOÒD ISLAND (1969), which also featured very graphic sex. It inspired a sequel, BEAST OF BLOOD (1970). HORROR EXPRESS (1970), brought aboard a train by Christopher Lee, was met by Peter Cushing, but the force that turned victims into

"Vampire People", made in the Philippines

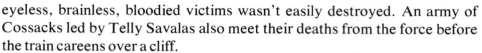

eyeless, brainless, bloodied victims wasn't easily destroyed. An army of Cossacks led by Telly Savalas also meet their deaths from the force before the train careens over a cliff.

BEAST OF THE YELLOW LIGHT (1971), THE INCREDIBLE TWO-HEADED TRANSPLANT (1971), THE THING WITH TWO HEADS, and Columbia's THE MUTATIONS followed, along with THE BLOOD WATERS OF DR. Z, THE WEREWOLF OF WASHINGTON, THE BOY WHO CRIED WEREWOLF, and LADY FRANKENSTEIN. Prehistoric life was depicted in Hammer's ONE MILLION B.C. (1966), with lovely Raquel Welch sporting the first cave bikini. Hammer continued its prehistoric trend with LOST CONTINENT (1968), SLAVE GIRLS (1968), WHEN DINOSAURS RULED THE EARTH (1970), and CREATURES THE WORLD FORGOT (1971). The latter two featured incredibly beautiful cave girls and a large amount of sex. Edgar Rice Burroughs' tales were given film treatment, THE LAND THAT TIME FORGOT and AT THE EARTH'S CORE (1976) recounting the adventures of David Innes in Pelucidar. Black exploitation-horror films, such as Pamela Grier's PANTHER GIRL and Bernie Casey in DR. BLACK AND MR. HYDE, were also released in 1976.

Townspeople fleeing in terror from "The Great Spider Invasion"

*Leslie Banks as the villain in "The Most Dangerous Game",
courtesy of Janus Films*

chapter 4

MAD DOCTORS,
MAD SCIENTISTS,
AND HEAVIES

THIS AREA OF FILM HORROR is large enough for an entire chapter and comparable to its predecessors, the beasts, monsters, and ghouls of the thirties horror classics. It concerns the human monster, which arose from the dark laboratories that produced monstrous creations. The area of the human monster consists of three branches: the pre-sci-fi-oriented adventure, which involves villains and cads who create horror out of desire for the hero's virgin girlfriend, money, power, or even revenge for a past injustice; the sci-fi-oriented serials, which differed in style and motivation from the old-house thrillers in that the villains weren't content with abducting the girl or obtaining the will of an eccentric millionaire but sought world conquest or destruction; the post-sci-fi psychodrama, in which mentally disturbed murderers turned to criminality out of jealousy, desire, envy, poverty, vengeance, or insecurity and showed an ever-increasing delight in sadism, sexual abuse, and bloodletting, with no motivation other than an insane desire for murder.

The 1920s took a look at the deranged horror of the human monster with Robert Weine's THE CABINET OF DR. CALIGARI, starring Werner Krauss as Caligari, who creates a sleepwalking fiend, Cesare (Conrad Veidt). Caligari is the head of an insane asylum and in a diary he reveals that he mimics a true-to-life man who placed a somnambulist under his control to kill for him. Hans Janowitz' script comes from an actual case history of a German murderer. The set designs are nightmarish, depicting the mind of an insane man. Prior to this film, Abel Gance's MADNESS OF DR. TUBE (1915) used a distorted-set motif to depict a madman's mind. Lon Chaney, Sr. appeared in THE PENALTY, (1920), THE SHOCK, and A BLIND BARGAIN, in the latter playing a mad scientist as well as the result of his endeavors, an ape-man. THE BELLS portrayed Lon as a killer, while THE MONSTER cast him as mad Dr. Ziska.

DR. MABUSE (1922), a German film directed by Fritz Lang, showed Mabuse (Rudolph Klein Rogge) as a damning villain plotting to throw the world into economic chaos with his counterfeit money. He exploits a decadent populace instead of rebuilding it. Gustav Von Sefferitz' role as Mr. Grimes in SPARROWS (1926) was also motivated by money and power. He steals money from a band of poverty-stricken mothers who entrust their wards to him to raise on his farm. He has other plans and sells them as child laborers. THE MAGICIAN (1926) featured Paul Wegener in a Somerset Maugham story directed by Rex Ingram. The tale concerns an alchemist who discovers the secret of life. Part of the formula's ingredient lies in virgin heroine Alice Terry. She is subsequently abducted and bound and awaits her fate until the hero intervenes and saves her. THE WIZARD (1927) saw Von Sefferitz in another villainous role as a mad doctor out to get revenge against his son's murderers with an apeman. WAXWORKS (1924) and HANDS OF ORLAC followed suit in presenting murder for revenge motifs.

Universal's THE MAN WHO LAUGHS (1925) was based on a Victor Hugo tale about Gwynplaine (Conrad Veidt), whose face is contorted into a horrible fixed grin as a result of vengeance against his father by a band of evil men. THE OLD DARK HOUSE (1933), was based on a novel by J.B. Priestly and directed in a neat old-house-thriller style by James Whale. The cast, including Boris Karloff as a murderous butler, assembles in an eerie mansion. Paramount's MURDER BY THE CLOCK (1931) was unique in presenting the screen's killer—lovely, lethal Lilyan Tishman. Paramount's ISLAND OF LOST SOULS (1932) was based on H.G. Wells' *The Island of Doctor Moreau*. Directed by Ernest Kenton, the film's heavy, Charles Laughton, is a mad

Dame Flora Robson and friend discover a victim of
"The Beast in the Cellar"

doctor involved in evolution research. He attempts to mate animals with humans through vivisection. His greatest achievement, so he believes, is to mate a panther girl with hero Richard Arlen, which, he hopes, will reinstate his position in London. On the other hand, Count Zaroff (Leslie Banks) never wishes to return to the civilization that alienated him from his island to hunt THE MOST DANGEROUS GAME. This 1932 RKO film was directed by Ernest B. Schoedsak and Irving Pichel from the story by Richard Connell. Zaroff's mania to hunt humans down like animals is illuminated by his prizes exhibited on wall plaques in the trophy room. Fay Wray is the prize Zaroff desires to win after he hunts Rainsforth (Joel McCrea), an excellent hunter of big game himself. The two play an excellent game of cat-and-mouse in the dense trappings of the mist-shrouded island. Zaroff is destroyed by a pack of bloodhounds in the finale, leaving the hero and heroine speeding away from the doomed island on a boat.

The thirties thriller continued with Barrymore's MAD GENIUS (1931), a remake of Dr. Mabuse. Lionel Atwill was cast as mad DOCTOR X (1932), who had a mania for researching synthetic flesh. Todd Browning's FREAKS enact murder out of revenge for the death of their fellow friend and freak. Universal cast Bela Lugosi as mad Doctor Mirakle in MURDERS IN THE RUE MORGUE. Director Robert Florey achieves many thrills throughout, but none match the mad doctor's murder of a streetwalker, played by Arlene Francis. The prostitute is tied to a makeshift cross and bled to death as she tries to escape her doom, shown on shadows cast upon the dungeon wall. Her cries die out and her body is left floating in the river. Lionel Atwill returned as an enraged husband who kills his wife's lovers with zoo animals in Paramount's MURDERS IN THE ZOO (1932). The following year brought Boris Karloff as Professor Moriant's reincarnated horror in THE GHOUL.

MYSTERY IN THE WAX MUSEUM (1933) cast Lionel Atwill as a mad murderer whose charred face, hidden behind a mask of wax, was broken away by near victim Fay Wray in one of horror's most exciting moments. THE RAVEN (1935) was inspired by Poe. Bela Lugosi is cast as mad Doctor Vollin, who invents a variety of torture instruments, which he puts to use on Irene Ware's family. Her father and her suitor resent Vollin's obsession with her, only to wind up almost victims on a platter of death. Boris Karloff is cast as an escaped criminal that Vollin disfigures so he can aid the madman in his plot to abduct Irene and slay her family. M (1931) cast Peter Lorre

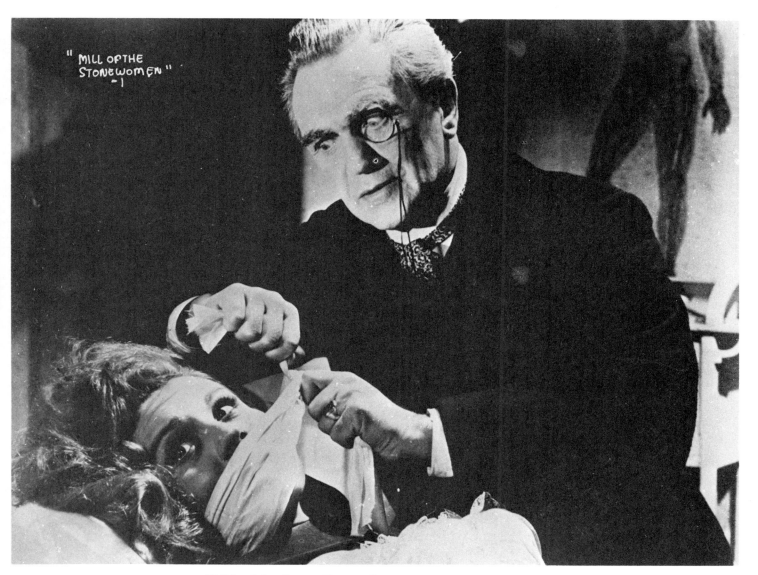

"Mill of the Stone Women", one of the earliest horror films

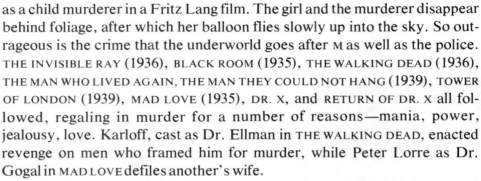

as a child murderer in a Fritz Lang film. The girl and the murderer disappear behind foliage, after which her balloon flies slowly up into the sky. So outrageous is the crime that the underworld goes after M as well as the police. THE INVISIBLE RAY (1936), BLACK ROOM (1935), THE WALKING DEAD (1936), THE MAN WHO LIVED AGAIN, THE MAN THEY COULD NOT HANG (1939), TOWER OF LONDON (1939), MAD LOVE (1935), DR. X, and RETURN OF DR. X all followed, regaling in murder for a number of reasons—mania, power, jealousy, love. Karloff, cast as Dr. Ellman in THE WALKING DEAD, enacted revenge on men who framed him for murder, while Peter Lorre as Dr. Gogal in MAD LOVE defiles another's wife.

The second branch of horror exhibited by the human monster comes out of the sci-fi-oriented Saturday-afternoon serials of the forties and early fifties. The serial dominated filmfare for a decade, the reasons for its success simple. Viewers were offered an action-dominated story with a simple plot that infused science fiction with mad doctors and mad scientists. During World War II producers interjected Nazi agents, Japanese heavies, and others who extorted money for the axis powers and blew up warehouses, munitions plants, and factories producing war-related materials.

THE CLUTCHING HAND (1936) was a doctor who sought a vast cache of money by faking a discovery of synthetic gold. SOS COAST GUARD (1937) had Bela Lugosi as the heavy trying to supply a foreign power with a deadly gas. SECRET OF TREASURE ISLAND (1938) had a professor manufacturing death bombs. FLYING G MEN (1939) battled enemy spies. Republic's MYSTERIOUS DR. SATAN was Eduardo Cianelli, who robbed banks with the aid of a robot in this 1940 outing. Bela Lugosi's Dr. Zorka was aided in creating weapons by an evil-looking robot in THE PHANTOM CREEPS (1939). SPY SMASHER (1942) was a typical stylized forties serial, as was G MEN VS THE BLACK DRAGON (1943). Nazis abounded in JUNGLE QUEEN (1945) while Roy Barcroft, with the aid of a transformation machine, became an evil pirate in MANHUNT OF MYSTERY ISLAND (1945). THE PURPLE MONSTER (1945) concerned an alien who sought to take over the world. THE CRIMSON GHOST (1946) was after a Cyclotrode machine stolen from the government by his murderous brigand. Horrid femme fatales also became increasingly popular in serials, as evidenced by THE BLACK WIDOW (1947). The evil Sombra the Spiderwoman was out to steal a vital rocket formula that her father required in order to dominate the world. Typical plot silliness that dominated these cliffhanging thril-

Viveca Lindfors is an artist-murderer in "Cauldron of Blood"

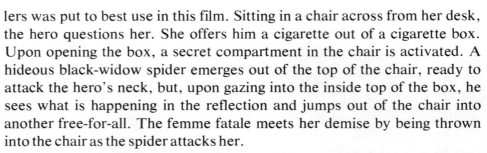

lers was put to best use in this film. Sitting in a chair across from her desk, the hero questions her. She offers him a cigarette out of a cigarette box. Upon opening the box, a secret compartment in the chair is activated. A hideous black-widow spider emerges out of the top of the chair, ready to attack the hero's neck, but, upon gazing into the inside top of the box, he sees what is happening in the reflection and jumps out of the chair into another free-for-all. The femme fatale meets her demise by being thrown into the chair as the spider attacks her.

THE INVISIBLE MONSTER (1950) was another supervillain who planned to rule the world with a superinvisibility formula. CANADIAN MOUNTIES VS THE ATOMIC INVADERS (1953) further mixed sci fi with the popularized cliffhanging serial. Monogram's CHAMBER OF HORRORS featured Leslie Banks, while Paramount's MAD DOCTOR OF MARKET STREET offered Lionel Atwill. Boris Karloff became Dr. Blair in Columbia's DEVIL COMMANDS, obsessed with bringing back his wife's spirit. HUMAN MONSTER, DEAD MEN WALK, DEAD EYES OF LONDON, PICTURE OF DORIAN GRAY (1945), and STRANGLER OF THE SWAMP followed. In the latter Rosemary LaPlanche was menaced by a mysterious strangler near a mist-shrouded marsh. The forties also brought portrayals of Bluebeard, with John Carradine as the artist who murdered Parisian ladies. BLUEBEARD is cast as a puppet maker who performs street shows. Laird Cregar depicted the infamous Saucy Jack in the well-done THE LODGER with Merle Oberon.

The fifties killer was motivated by love, lust, power, greed, and revenge for a past indignity, with a very conservative dose of sex added. HOUSE OF WAX (1953) starred Vincent Price as Henry Jarrod, who was beaten by his partner and left for dead in a burning wax shop. In THE MAZE (1953) an heir was turned into a frog. Price returned in an evil role as Columbia's MAD MAGICIAN, motivated by his wife's unfaithfulness. BLACK SLEEP regaled in murder. MACABRE (1955) offered a gimmick to viewers. The audience would be given a free $1,000 life-insurance policy against dying by fright. The film concerned a father's efforts to locate his missing daughter, who was buried alive. MGM's LIZZIE and SCREAMING MIMI mixed murder with sex, conveyed beautifully by Anita Ekberg in the latter film. Boris Karloff became the HAUNTED STRANGLER (1958). HORRORS OF THE BLACK MUSEUM (1958) set the stage for a growing list of sadist fare. Michael Gough is cast as a crime writer whose murder stories are committed by him. Typi-

The Count entertains thoughts other than blood-drinking when he sees the captured maiden

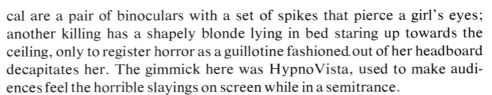

cal are a pair of binoculars with a set of spikes that pierce a girl's eyes; another killing has a shapely blonde lying in bed staring up towards the ceiling, only to register horror as a guillotine fashioned out of her headboard decapitates her. The gimmick here was HypnoVista, used to make audiences feel the horrible slayings on screen while in a semitrance.

The sixties films provided viewers with supposed insights into the mind of a psychopathic killer in such fare as Roman Polanski's KNIFE IN THE WATER, REPULSION, and ANATOMY OF A PSYCHO, to name a few. Alfred Hitchcock's PSYCHO (1960) offers insight into the motivation of a psychopath. Anthony Perkins is Norman, a victim of an obsessive mother whose corpse he keeps rotting in the basement. Norman has a dual personality: he becomes his mother and dresses up to kill those who threaten his wellbeing—in this case Janet Leigh. In one of the screen's most shocking sequences Miss Leigh is sadistically slaughtered while taking a shower in the Bates Motel. The mother's personality completely takes Norman over by the last reel, as, sitting in an asylum, he relates to himself how clever he was in letting the police think that he, the mother, is responsible, thereby saving her son from being convicted of murder. In PSYCHOMANIA a disturbed Korean War veteran stabs nude models who pose for him until it is revealed that his sister is the actual killer. She loves him and was motivated by her insecurity to kill other girls around him. THE HYPNOTIC EYE gave viewers HypnoMagic in a sixties film with Jacques Bergerac as a hypnotist who makes people commit indignities upon themselves. CIRCUS OF HORRORS, and FACE OF TERROR both featured increased sadism, as did FLESH AND FIENDS, THE HAND, and HOMICIDAL. The latter 1961 William Castle film offered viewers the gimmick of a Fright Warning prior to the climax, asking viewers that couldn't take it to leave before the ending.

DR. BLOOD'S COFFIN starred Keiron Moore as a researcher causing numerous deaths; similar was CORRIDORS OF BLOOD, and HANDS OF A STRANGER followed. THE MILL OF STONE WOMEN was a gory tale about girls being tortured to death and exhibited in a museum as stone artwork. CREATURE WITH THE BLUE HAND featured a homicidal maniac, while INN OF THE FRIGHTENED PEOPLE employed a revenge-for-rape motif. PEEPING TOM (1959) depicted voyeurism as a motif for murder. The film shows a young man's obsession with pornography and with a desire to record fear on female victims' faces prior to murdering them. Bill Castle's 1958 shocker

A flesh-crawling scene from "Invasion of the Blood Farmers"

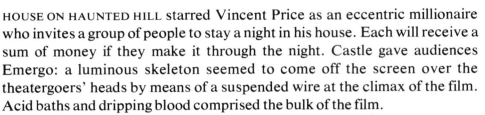

HOUSE ON HAUNTED HILL starred Vincent Price as an eccentric millionaire who invites a group of people to stay a night in his house. Each will receive a sum of money if they make it through the night. Castle gave audiences Emergo: a luminous skeleton seemed to come off the screen over the theatergoers' heads by means of a suspended wire at the climax of the film. Acid baths and dripping blood comprised the bulk of the film.

Lopert's HORROR CHAMBER OF DR. FAUSTUS (1960) inspired a wave of bloody torture flicks. This film concerns a doctor's efforts to turn his daughter's face into a beautiful thing. The film is mixed with rather gory sequences of surgical manipulation that show facial skin being grafted. It inspired other sadist-oriented films such as THE AWFUL DR. ORLOFF, who also tried to restore his daughter's good looks. THE HORRIBLE DR. HITCHCOCK starred Robert Flemyng and Barbara Steele in another dual-sister role. BLACK ZOO involved a murderer who used caged animals as instruments of death. THE CRAWLING HAND, MADMAN OF MANDERAS (1963), DUNGEON OF HORRORS, and BLOOD AND LACE all featured murderous goings on. DEMENTIA 13 was an AIP 1963 film about axe murders. A gimmick provided audiences with a D-13 test prior to entering the theater.

Warner's WHATEVER HAPPENED TO BABY JANE (1962) was Bob Aldrich's attempt at a Gothic chiller in grand-guignol style. SHOCK CORRIDOR told of an asylum terrorizer. THE THING WITHOUT A FACE depicted a pyromaniac's obsession. Bill Castle put Joan Crawford into a STRAITJACKET in a 1964 fright film about an axe murderess. The femme fatale's clients are people who pose a threat to her upcoming marriage. The killer turns out to be Joan Crawford's daughter, who wishes all to believe it is her mother Lucy who is the killer. Victor Buono was cast as THE STRANGLER (1964), also motivated by a domineering mother. Buono is a murdering lab technician obsessed with kewpie dolls. In Woolner's HORROR CASTLE Rosana Podesta is menaced by the Nuremberg killer, a psycho who abducts lovely women and tortures them to death. In one sequence a girl's cries and moans, coming from an iron maiden, grow silent as blood fills the receptacle at the bottom of the torture device. Another sequence shows a woman abducted and told that she will be abused and killed. The next sequence shows the pitiful creature tied to a chair as a cage is placed over her head with a carnivorous rat inside. Rosanna discovers that her husband Max may be involved and investigates, only to wind up tied to a table and about to be surgically operated

A rapist attacks in "Whirlpool"

on by a demented product of Nazi experimentation. The killer's face is a bloody half-skeletal thing with barely enough skin to be recognizable. Christopher Lee also starred. HUSH HUSH SWEET CHARLOTTE was another Bob Aldrich vehicle. Paramount cast Olivia De Haviland as an invalid in a stalled elevator in their offering LADY IN A CAGE. She was at the mercy of vicious youths, one of whom was James Caan, who go about ravaging the household. 2000 MANIACS from Box Office Spectaculars was a gory flick about a Southern town still seeking vengeance on Northerners for the Civil War. Just as bloody was BLOOD FEAST (1966), about young women being vivisected and having their organs made into an elixir of life. In the late sixties and early seventies box-office horror was turning more and more to sex and violence.

Some films offered crazed artists slaughtering people. This trend started with AIP's 1959 film BUCKET OF BLOOD. The crazed artist decapitated people with buzz saws, strangled nude girls, and put their corpses into posterity with plaster-of-paris molds. Some artists slashed victims and kept them in cold storage! Christopher Lee starred in THE TORTURE CHAMBER OF DR. SADISM, a very rarely seen film. Tallulah Bankhead was a Bible-toting fanatic in FANATIC or DIE DIE MY DARLING (1964). Stephanie Powers is her daughter in-law, whom she blames for her son's demise. She tries to rehabilitate her accursed soul through starvation and torture. Other psychothrillers to follow were: PARANOIA, MANIAC, HYSTERIA (1964), and SCREAM OF FEAR (1960) with Susan Strasberg.

TERROR IN THE HAUNTED HOUSE (1961) offered viewers Psychorama, which was nothing more than the appearance of a skull prior to a scene of horror. A similar warning of horrors was found in Warner's CHAMBER OF HORRORS (1966). The film used a horn and red flasher to warn viewers of an upcoming terror-filled moment. Amicus' THE SKULL (1965) was that of the Marquis de Sade and instilled murderous designs on those who possessed it. Paramount's THE MAD EXECUTIONERS completed the double bill. This German film was about a band of hooded killers who tortured, maimed, and killed lovely female victims. Christopher Lee was RASPUTIN THE MAD MONK a 1965 film from Hammer. Filmgoers were given Rasputin beards for attending. Other psycho offerings were Joey Heatherton and Troy Donahue in MY BLOOD RUNS COLD (1966), TWO ON A GUILLOTINE, and BERSERK, which featured Joan Crawford amidst a circus filled with mysterious murders,

"Crucible of Horror"

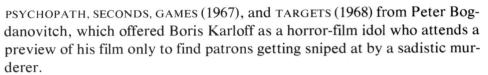

PSYCHOPATH, SECONDS, GAMES (1967), and TARGETS (1968) from Peter Bog-danovitch, which offered Boris Karloff as a horror-film idol who attends a preview of his film only to find patrons getting sniped at by a sadistic murderer.

Bette Davis was a femme fatale in both THE NANNY (1965) and THE ANNIVERSARY. Howard Vernon returned in another mad-doctor role, THE DIABOLICAL DR. Z (1967). This time he is aided by a girl who sadistically tortures female victims with a machine. AIP's MILLION EYES OF SUMURU featured Shirley Eaton, the golden girl of 007's GOLDFINGER, as the leader of a feminist organization that takes the rather radical approach to equal rights of killing males. A typical sequence shows a man strangled to death by a big-bosomed amazon, who locks his head between her legs while grinding her hips! THE EMBALMER (1969) was a necrophile who abducts pretty Italian chicks. Similar was THE MANCHESTER MORGUE (1974) and BODY STEALERS (1969). AIP's SCREAM AND SCREAM AGAIN (1970) offered Vincent Price's tale about reproducing androids with murder victims. Christopher Lee also starred. Price joined forces with Peter Cushing in MADHOUSE (1974). The run of mad-doctor pictures ended with AIP's Vincent Price character in THE ABOMINABLE DR. PHIBES and DR. PHIBES RISES AGAIN.

The psychokillers of the seventies exploded on the screen with a liberal dosing of sex, violence, and gore motivated by no other reason than satisfying a whim! Cinemation's FROM EAR TO EAR (1971) showed a group of females horribly torturing a female deaf-mute. National Genral's CAT O'NINE TAILS is a mystery set in Italy. LETS SCARE JESSICA TO DEATH, a 1971 Paramount film, had a woman believing that her friends all met death at the hands of a vampire. On a less bloody note but equally chilling were UA's WHATS THE MATTER WITH HELEN, AUNT ALICE with Ruth Gordon, Tigron's BEAST IN THE CELLAR, THE KILLING OF SISTER GEORGE, BLOOD AND LACE, BARON BLOOD (1972), and Columbia's CREEPING FLESH. NMD's INVASION OF THE BLOOD FARMERS told of a Druid cult that drained victims of blood with a pump in an effort to revive their dying queen. Jerry Gross' WHIRLPOOL told of a sexual psychopath.

Hallmark was emerging as the leader in blood and gore, as evidenced by their MARK OF THE DEVIL, which boasted that it was rated V for violent and distributed vomit bags to patrons. Their LAST HOUSE ON THE LEFT is a 1973 ripoff of Bergman's VIRGIN SPRING. Two young girls are picked up on

The crazed butcher on the loose in "Torso", courtesy J. Brenner Assoc.

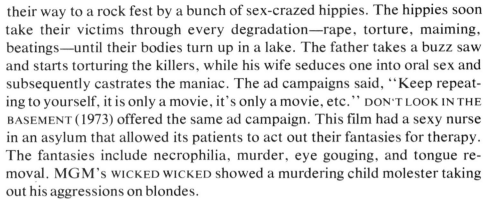

their way to a rock fest by a bunch of sex-crazed hippies. The hippies soon take their victims through every degradation—rape, torture, maiming, beatings—until their bodies turn up in a lake. The father takes a buzz saw and starts torturing the killers, while his wife seduces one into oral sex and subsequently castrates the maniac. The ad campaigns said, "Keep repeating to yourself, it is only a movie, it's only a movie, etc." DON'T LOOK IN THE BASEMENT (1973) offered the same ad campaign. This film had a sexy nurse in an asylum that allowed its patients to act out their fantasies for therapy. The fantasies include necrophilia, murder, eye gouging, and tongue removal. MGM's WICKED WICKED showed a murdering child molester taking out his aggressions on blondes.

Some fantasy murder films, much less horrible and more campy, some outright spoofs, came from England. Christopher Lee's adaptation of Sax Rohmner's Fu Manchu character emerged in the sixties: FACE OF, BRIDES OF, CASTLE OF, AND HORROR OF FU MANCHU: with Lee excellent as the villain always outwitted by Scotland Yard's Neyland Smith. UA's THEATER OF BLOOD cast Vincent Price as Edward Lionheart a Shakespearean actor who does in critics that mock his performances with Shakespearean murders. Other rather good murder fare were 1974's TOYS AREN'T FOR CHILDREN and FOUR FLIES ON GREY VELVET. One of the best seventies films on the subject came from Hitchcock: FRENZY told of a necktie strangler who was terrorfying London. Barbara Leigh Hunt plays the owner of a dating service that the killer enters. Hitchcock's style is shown best here when the killer tells her his preferences in a kinky date. She registers increasing horror as the killer assaults and strangles her while she sits in her chair. The second slaying we see in progress. The innocent victim meets the killer and walks him up to her flat. The camera follows the couple up the staircase, through the room, and out the window, panning to the streets below. The murder takes place off-screen but is much more effective, as the silence of the flat changes to the busy, noisy street below.

WHATEVER BECAME OF JACK AND JILL (1974), CRESCENDO, FRIGHT, and THE PENTHOUSE followed. HANDS OF THE RIPPER (1961) from Hammer showed Jack slicing up a topless victim. NIGHT WATCH (1974) was more restrained and more mysterious, with Liz Taylor witnessing a murder and not being believed by hubby Laurence Harvey, who is playing around with neighbor Billie De Whitlaw. AIP's SISTERS was a Brian De Palma outing

Graphic violence in "Beast of Blood"

about two sisters, one a good girl and the other a dangerous maniac who stabs her lover and is later found out to be one and the same as her good nemesis. Hallmark continued to provide gore with such films as SLAUGHTER HOTEL, APARTMENT ON THE 13th FLOOR, HOUSE THAT VANISHED, and DON'T LOOK OUT THE WINDOW (1976). The latter film was made under the titles THE LIVING DEAD AT THE MANCHESTER MORGUE and BREAKFAST AT THE MANCHESTER MORGUE, a ripoff of NIGHT OF THE LIVING DEAD. Director Jorge Grau also made BLOOD CEREMONY. SCREAM BLOODY MURDER was claimed to be so shocking and gore-filled that viewers were told to employ a blindfold given away at theaters. Box Offices' PLEASE DON'T EAT MY MOTHER followed, along with TWITCH OF THE DEATH NERVE. THE CASE OF THE SMILING STIFFS, GARDEN OF THE DEAD, DERANGED, SILENT NIGHT BLOODY NIGHT, Bryanston's A KNIFE FOR THE LADIES, SAVAGE SISTERS, and AIP's CANNIBAL GIRLS (1973) added to the growing trend of gruesomeness.

LA GRANDE TROUILLE was a 1974 outing with Peter Cushing, who plays an old horror actor who takes up romantic films. The producer plans an evening he won't forget, with pretty girls being cut in half, axe killings, and disfigurement. SEIZURE, RAZOR IN THE FLESH, and Bava's HATCHET FOR A HONEYMOON followed. The latter Spanish—Italian horror film was about a man who axes women on their wedding nights. KILL KILL KILL, BLOOD, BLOOD-SPLATTERED BRIDE, THE MAD BUTCHER, THE FLESH AND BLOOD SHOW, and TORSO had sex and gore killings. Bryanston's TEXAS CHAINSAW MASSACRE had a maniac going about the countryside with a buzz saw. SPASMO (1976) is about a kinky ladykiller with an appetite spiced with whips, ladies' undergarments, and daggers. Mahler's KILLER SNAKES were used by a young man who was also a sex-hungry sadist. DEEP RED, also from Mahler, casts David Hemmings in a gore-filled horror tale. TENDER FLESH is a 1976 Brut production based on a story by Jack Gross and Wallace C. Bennett. Cannibalism sets the scene for this perverse shocker, which concerns a girl's efforts to prove to the local police that a couple practices cannibalism in their own home. SNUFF is another totally perverse shocker, which boasted in ad campaigns that it was "filmed in South America where life is cheap." The film tells of an insane group who make their victim pretend to die in a film, only to have her realize that she is actually being slaughtered and disemboweled on film.

*Gunnor Hassen plays Leatherface, a crazed killer who wears a flesh mask as
he poses with his 100 year-old grandfather in "The Texas Chain Saw Massacre",
a Bryanston release*

chapter 5

THAT OLD BLACK MAGIC

VOODOO WHILE ACTIVE IN HAITI, never really came to life as a source of screen horror until 1932. The screen up to this time was dominated by the old-house thriller and the birth of the Universal horror machine. Horror wasn't much inspired by voodoo, since the audience found it silly and laughable while the producers found it limited in story. Most voodoo films looked very similar in scope to other films on the same subject. Universal made the first and possibly the best film on the subject, with Bela Lugosi as M. Legendre, WHITE ZOMBIE (1932). Directed by Victor Halperin, the film conveys eeriness and gloom in excellent atmospheric sets. Garnett Weston's screenplay unfolds with a woman's arrival in Haiti to meet her fiancée. While aboard the ship that carried her she met a wealthy man called Beaumont, who secretly desires to make her his slave. He joins forces with voodoo master M. Legendre, who steals her shawl and fashions a waxen image of the victim. Casting it into flames, her fate is sealed. While at a dinner party at Beaumont's estate she is toasted but upon looking into her glass sees Legendre's hideous face and dies. She is placed in a crypt, after which her corpse is stolen. Legendre plans a double-cross and also makes Madeline his slave, as he wishes her to work on his sugar plantation. Her spouse joins forces with a missionary, who knocks Legendre over a cliff, where his army of living dead are besetting the hero. Legendre's unconsciousness in turn causes his army to walk over the edge to their deaths below. Meanwhile Beaumont attacks Legendre, also causing the two to fall to their deaths below, and the spell on Madeline (Madge Bellamy) is lifted. The film has many assets, among them the direction, photography, and script. The photography by Arthur Martinelli is rich and mellow, best shown in sequences with the zombies walking aimlessly about the countryside.

Director Victor Halperin went on to make REVOLT OF THE ZOMBIES (1936), while Monogram studios made low-budget fare such as CORPSE

VANISHES (1942), KING OF THE ZOMBIES (1941), and REVENGE OF THE ZOMBIES (1943). Val Lewton's I WALKED WITH A ZOMBIE, made for RKO in 1943, was done in the classic, subtle Lewton approach, with the horror off-screen and up to the audience's imagination. CULT OF THE COBRA (1955) had a bunch of army buddies cursed for taking a picture of a girl transforming into a cobra. Her vengeance followed the men back to the states, where she seduced and killed each one. Boris Karloff appeared in Universal's boring VOODOO ISLAND with Beverly Tyler.

Some filmmakers mixed the power of voodoo with love, one of the results of which was CRY OF THE BEWITCHED (1957), wherein a girl puts the whammy on her lover, a plantation owner. THE DISEMBODIED (1957) showed Allison Hayes putting a spell on her man, while VOODOO WOMAN (1957) had lovely Marla English putting a hex on Mike Connors. ZOMBIES OF MORA TAU (1957) guarded buried treasure. The following year Richard Boone played a cemetery owner who discovered that he could kill by putting pins into gravesites on a map in I BURY THE LIVING. MACUMBA LOVE followed in 1960, along with WAR OF THE ZOMBIES (1963), TEENAGE ZOMBIES, ATOMIC BRAIN, ASTRO ZOMBIES, and FOUR SKULLS OF JONATHAN DRAKE with Valerie French. PLAGUE OF THE ZOMBIES (1966) gave viewers a gimmick in Zombie glasses, given out to audiences and put on to avoid getting cursed and spotted by zombies. Mexico sent across the border INVASION OF THE ZOMBIES, DR. SATAN (1966), DR. SATAN VS BLACK MAGIC, SANTO VS BLACK MAGIC (1972), INCREDIBLE PROFESSOR ZOVECK (1971), and THE INVASION OF THE DEAD.

THE OBLONG BOX (1961) was directed by Gordon Hessler for AIP and starred Vincent Price and Christopher Lee as twin brothers. Lee becomes a maniac after undergoing voodoo rites from natives who have mistaken him for Price, who killed a little boy with his stallion. Hessler enhances the climax by not showing Lee's disfigured face until the end. Cinemation's double bill of gore was I EAT YOUR SKIN and I DRINK YOUR BLOOD (1971). The first film has a mad scientist on a voodoo-infested island creating zombies from dead people's sera and mixing it with radioactivity to create zombie reptiles! The latter film has blood-crazed hippies running loose killing and maiming innocent victims. The CORPSE GRINDERS were customers at a diner served up as kidney pies; a Miss Chicken is served on the menu as breasts and legs. THE MEPHISTO WALTZ plagued pianist Alan Alda, while SNAKE PEOPLE (1971) plagued local natives, led by Boris Karloff, with cobra venom. AIP's SUGAR HILL was a 1975 black-exploitation film with pretty Marki Bey, who got vengeance on the underworld for snuffing her husband with her brigand of living dead. PSYCHIC KILLER (1976) killed victims mentally, while J.D.'S REVENGE possessed the soul of a man to get vengeance for him in another 1976 horror film, this one for AIP.

An old advertisement for a horror film

chapter 6

THREE

CLASSIC HORROR FILMS

THE FIELD OF HORROR has provided many entertaining moments. The genre has produced a few classic films, most from the golden age of cinema and all just as frightening today as when they were first seen by millions of avid fans, unexcelled in style, direction, atmosphere, and screenplay: THE PHANTOM OF THE OPERA (1925), THE HUNCHBACK OF NOTRE DAME (1923), and DR. JEKYLL AND MR. HYDE (1932).

Universal's THE PHANTOM was based on Gaston Leroux' novel and brought to the screen by producer Carl Laemmle. Rupert Julien's direction of this Gothic-style romance brings the film more than horror. It is indeed a mystery, a love story, a serial, and a blend of fairytale and horror. What follows is the actual filmography.

At the Paris Opera House a gala performance is in the works. Meanwhile, a strange deal is being negotiated in the executive office. It is being sold without a warning to the buyer about the spirit that resides there. In the shadows we see the shadow of an eerie-looking man. A group of chorus girls are frightened by the figure. One remarks that the figure had no nose. Another remarks, "His ghastly eyes are beads in which there is no light. His skin is leperous parchment stretched over bones." (Raymond Shrecks' screenplay brings out the eerie quality of the incident, shown in the catacombs and dark passages under the Opera.) Bouquet, a stagehand, says he first saw the figure in a dock on stage three: "A flash of shadow and he was gone.'' The Phantom (Lon Chaney, Sr.) sends a letter to Christine Dane (Mary Philbin) saying it is she who will star in the Opera's gala production and not Carlotta (Virginia Pearson). Raoul (Norman Kerry) goes to Miss Dane's room after the performance, where the voice of the Phantom speaks to her through a secret panel. He urges her to sing and be truly great. He sends a letter edged in black to Carlotta as a warning not to take the lead. But, encouraged by her mother to play Marguerite, she does, only to die under a chandelier sent crashing to the stage by Erik the Phantom. The Opera's Phantom seizes Christine and spirits her away through dark catacombs to an underground lair, where he resides. "Look not upon my face mask,'' he claims. "If I am a Phantom, it is because man's hatred has made me so.'' With that she faints on a bed and awakens to rip off his mask while he sits at his organ. This classic sequence is one of the first horror moments to occur in the film. Erik's mishappen head, blazing eyes, and upturned nostrils combine to make him look like a living skull: "Feast your eyes, glut your soul on my accursed ugliness!'' Proving his desire for her, he lets her go to sing one last time: "Remember, if the two of you are together, it will be death to the both of you,'' he warns. At the masked ball he appears as a figure clad in red. Christine meets Raoul on the roof. They make plans to leave the country, but Erik overhears them. At 9 P.M. the barouche stops at the rotunda side of the Opera house. Joseph, a stagehand, is found murdered and Christine is abducted by Erik. Ledroux (Arthur Edmund Carewe) of the secret police aids Raoul in locating the Phantom. The towering catacombs loom overhead as the two seek him. The Phantom, meanwhile, is watching them via a secret panel. He tells Christine, "Now see evil spirits make evil faces, I will not be cheated out of my happiness.'' Ledroux and Raoul enter a chamber of fire in which Erik intends to roast them alive, but they escape their fate via a trapdoor, only to find themselves sealed up in a room with a keg of gunpowder. Erik goes berserk and asks Christine to choose her mate. Given a choice to save her rescuers, she must choose either scorpion or a grasshopper affixed to a chest. She chooses the scorpion, and Erik says she has just sentenced the two to drowning under torrents of water. A mob enters the chamber, causing Erik to flee with his captive in a coach. The coach overturns and the mob attacks Erik, throwing his battered body into the river. Christine is reunited with her beloved Raoul. Cinematographers Virgil Miller, Charles Van Enger, and Milt Bridenbecker excel thoughout the production. The lavish sets and eeri-

Lon Chaney as Erik, his most famous role, in "The Phantom of the Opera"

ness of the Opera combine to give one an excellent scenario for Chaney's excellent character. Other remakes never equalled the style of Chaney's Erik. A 1943 version offered Claude Rains, while Hammer's remake cast Herbert Lom. Brian De Palma made it into a parody in his 1974 version THE PHANTOM OF THE PARADOX.

THE HUNCHBACK OF NOTRE DAME (1923), also made by Universal, featured the talents of Chaney as Quasimodo, the mute, deformed bellringer of Victor Hugo's classic. Director Wallace Worsely shows Quasimodo as a tortured soul in love with a gypsy Esmerelda. She is loved by Jehan, who stabs his rival and places the blame on her. About to be publically executed, Quasimodo swings down to the crowd and carries her off to the top of the Notre Dame cathedral tower, where he wages a one-man war on those who would rescue her. Jehan enters the tower and stabs him, throwing his body to the streets of Paris below. The role was repeated by Charles Laughton in RKO's 1939 version, and by Anthony Quinn in the 1957 version. Both failed to equal the quality of the original, reflected in Worsely's direction and Chaney's ability to evoke sympathy and sadness from the viewer.

The third classic comes from the pen of Robert Louis Stevenson, DR. JEKYLL AND MR. HYDE. The novel was first filmed in 1912 but was popularized in the 1920 Paramount version with John Barrymore as the pin-headed, evil Mr. Hyde. Paramount's 1932 version with Frederick March was directed by Rouben Mamoulian and richly showed the Stevenson classic about a man's desire to separate good and evil. Hyde lusts after Ivy (Miriam Hopkins), who is desired also by Dr. Henry Jekyll, the alter ego. She rejects this side of the man, preferring to be ravished by the sexually motivated Mr. Hyde. Mamoulian brings to his film the concepts of Freud, for Jekyll's repressed ego Hyde harbors his sexuality. The cinematic interchanges into this creature provide the film's best imaginative moments. Spencer Tracy depicted the infamous pair in the 1941 version, also for Paramount, without the use of makeup. Universal turned the classic into a comedy with ABBOTT AND COSTELLO MEET DR. JEKYLL AND MR. HYDE (1953). The film took on total banality with Columbia's SON OF DR. JEKYLL (1951), DAUGHTER OF DR. JEKYLL (1957), HOUSE OF FRIGHT (1961), and I MONSTER (1970) with Christopher Lee. Hammer's DR. JEKYLL AND SISTER HYDE (1971) starred Ralph Bates and Martine Beswickas, his female ego. This Roy Ward Baker film is interesting in that the transformation is transsexual in nature.

chapter 7

GHOSTS AND HAUNTINGS

WHEN ONE THINKS IN TERMS of what is frightful and scary, one thinks of ghosts and spirits. This basic idea of what is scary is perhaps the least adapted to the screen, due in part to the treatment of a ghost story by the filmmaker and to the viewer, who reasons that what he cannot see can't frighten him as much as animated creations or other monstrous imagery. The ghost story has been the basis for many a comic film. Among famous comedians who came across spirits are Laurel and Hardy, Abbott and Costello, the Three Stooges, Bob Hope and Claudette Colbert, Martin and Lewis, and the Dead End Kids. Nevertheless, a few top-quality ghost stories did make it to celluloid, relying on speculation and implication rather than out-and-out camera trickery. George Melies started the ghost genre with his 1896 short, CAVE OF THE DEMONS. The film features his perfection of the double-exposure technique to simulate ghosts and apparitions. Other ghostly tales to follow were UNDRESSING EXTRAORDINAIRE, FAIRY OF THE BLACK ROCKS (1905) and HAUNTED CASTLE.

The Universal horror machine offered a mixture of science fiction and fright in H.G. Wells' THE INVISIBLE MAN (1933). Claude Rains—or rather, his voice—appeared as Jack Griffen. His body was kept invisible by a mysterious drug called onocaine. It had the added effect of inducing a slowly progressive paranoia. The film's spectacular special effects were done by master artist John P. Fulton. The most interesting bits came when Griffen emerges into a snowstorm and into a smoke-filled room. He removes his bandages, and as they come off, we see progressively less of him. The director, James Whale, saw fit to add a slight touch of humor, as he did with his BRIDE OF FRANKENSTEIN. The humor and Griffen's demented, maniacal speeches about taking over the world make the film succeed. Vincent Price also took off the bandages as THE INVISIBLE MAN RETURNS

(1942), and Jon Hall appeared in THE INVISIBLE MAN'S REVENGE (1944). A Mexican version was also made.

Paramount's THE UNINVITED (1944), with Ray Milland, was a serious film about ridding a house that a couple inherited of demons and spirits. DEAD OF NIGHT was perhaps the first anthology film, offering five separate tales of the supernatural. In *The Christmas Story* a young girl enters a room to comfort a crying little boy, only to discover that he is a spirit of a child who died years ago. *The Ventriloquist's Dummy* concerns an entertainer's dummy that exerts an evil influence over its owner, who talks in the dummy's voice while possessed. In *The Haunted Mirror* a couple buys an antique mirror haunted with the stately appearance of an old bedroom. The husband develops a mania and finds himself completely dominated by the power of the mirror, which drives him to strangle his wife and slit his own throat. The film contains two other short tales of the supernatural.

Among other ghost films were: AIP's HEADLESS GHOST, ANGEL ON EARTH, (1961), GHOSTS OF ROME, which offered a little sex, GHOST OF DRAGSTRIP HOLLOW (1959), AUTOPSY OF A GHOST, Bill Castle's THIRTEEN GHOSTS for Columbia, complete with 3-D glasses, LIVING SKELETON (1968), and THE GHOST IN THE INVISIBLE BIKINI. Haunted houses were also shown in films such as HORROR HOUSE, HOUSE ON SKULL MOUNTAIN, and Japan's SNAKE GIRL AND THE SILVER-HAIRED WITCH. DR. DEATH, SEEKER OF SOULS (1973) was a mad doctor who killed his patients, while PHANTOM OF SOHO (1973) was an evildoer in a black hooded cape. THE OTHER (1972), based on the novel by Tom Tryon, took a serious look at possession, as did POSSESSION OF JOEL DELANEY (1973) with Shirley MacLaine.

A few classic ghost films were THE INNOCENTS and MGM's THE HAUNTING (1963). The latter film concerns a group of psychic researchers investigating a house in New England called Hill House. The haunted house attacks the group with walls that cave in, flying chairs, and other assorted paraphernalia as it seeks to possess the soul of one of the group, Eleanor (Julie Harris).

AIP's DIE MONSTER DIE and THE SHUTTERED ROOM were based on stories by H.P. Lovecraft. The latter was a frightening Seven Arts production about an evil presence locked up in a room. Twentieth Century Fox remade THE HAUNTING in 1973 as THE LEGEND OF HELL HOUSE. The haunted house, Belasco Mansion, is haunted by the spirit of its sadistic owner. A psychic team is under attack, with the house seeking to claim one member, played by Pamela Franklin. The spirit of the house tries to possess her soul and body.

"The Curse of the Crying Woman"

Herbert Lom as the head of the "Asylum"

chapter 8

ASSORTED TALES

OF TERROR

EDGAR ALLEN POE was the undisputed master of the macabre, with count-
less stories that have found their way onto the screen. As Jules Verne
inspired the field of science fiction, Poe inspired the cinema of the macabre.
A derivative type is the anthology film, a compilation of short stories
introduced or pieced together by a central theme or character. A Poe-based
film is a period horror story: the action occurs in a specific period of time, in
most cases the era in which it is written, the eighteenth century. The
anthology film includes a wide variety of horror stories that take place in
either the past or the present. While the Poe films tell of misery and
suffering, catalepsy, madness, lust, adultery, alcoholism, and drug addiction, the anthology films are more high-spirited tales of monsters, ghosts,
demons, and other not so heavy antagonists. The anthology film is more
light-hearted and doesn't attempt to relate horror to the human condition, as
does Poe's work. HOUSE OF THE SEVEN GABLES (1940) was based on a
Nathaniel Hawthorne story, while FALL OF THE HOUSE OF USHER (1948) was
Poe-inspired. Both set the stage for more period horror films, Gothic in
style and atmosphere. DEAD OF NIGHT (1946) is truly the first anthology film
of supernatural tales; MANFISH (1956) is an anthology film composed of two
Poe works, *The Tell Tale Heart* and *The Gold Bug*.
American International Pictures, Vincent Price, and Roger Corman

combined talents to make some very good Poe-inspired tales in the early sixties. They proved financially successful for AIP and offered the horror buff a new genre source of horror—the Gothic classic. The first Poe-inspired tale was AIP's HOUSE OF USHER (1960), screenplayed by Richard Matheson and starring Vincent Price. Price is cast as Usher, a man who resists another's efforts to wed his sister. Usher feels that she is suffering from madness, which is actually catalepsy—the family history is riddled with it. His sister is placed in a crypt, but she escapes to get vengeance on her brother. The walls of the house cave in on the family, putting an end to their suffering and despair. PIT AND THE PENDULUM (1961) followed also from AIP with Vincent Price. Human misery is again shown, with Price cast as a wealthy madman obsessed with sadism. His lust for evil began as a child upon witnessing the torture murder of his mother at the hands of his father and uncle. This results in his brooding interest in torture, shown in a dungeon torture chamber beneath the castle. Price's sister is planning to drive him insane to acquire his money. Her greed brings death at the hands of her brother. TALES OF TERROR (1963) from AIP offered a trilogy. The first yarn is a combination of two Poe tales, *The Black Cat* and *The Cask of Amontillado*. Peter Lorre's addiction to drink results in his wife's extramarital affair, which in turn causes Lorre to murder his wife and her lover. *Morella*, the second tale, shows Vincent Price afflicted with alcoholism stemming from his necrophilia for his dead wife. Her spirit haunts her child as well as her spouse. *The Case of M. Valdemar*, the third tale, offers Vincent Price as a catatonic, the result of his wife's jealous lover, who blackmails her into loving him. Price rises to vent his revenge.

THE RAVEN (1963) teamed Lorre, Price, and Karloff in a colorful tale of terror. TWICE-TOLD TALES is an anthology based on Hawthorne's works. *Dr. Herdeggar's Experiment* shows Vincent Price afflicted with lust. His adulterous intentions are unknown to the victim, who loves his best friend. An enraged Price, unable to cope with her rejection, poisons the object of his illness and destroys himself. *Rappucinni's Daughter*, the second tale, has Price cast as an insane man motivated by his wife's desertion. Not wishing to pass his feelings of rejection and loneliness to others, he poisons his daughter.

AIP's PREMATURE BURIAL (1962) shows Ray Milland afflicted with insanity caused by his fear of being buried alive. HAUNTED PALACE (1964),

Peter Cushing as Gumsdyke in "Tales from the Crypt"

based on H.P. Lovecraft, offered Vincent Price in a tale of witchcraft. Far superior in story, settings, and talent (Price and Corman) was THE MASQUE OF THE RED DEATH. Charles Beaumont offers us an allegorical screenplay. Vincent Price is Prince Prospero, a debaucher and evil devil worshipper, who locks himself away in his castle and revels in horrid devil practices and orgies while the plague brings death to those outside. Red Death enters the festivities disguised as a fellow partygoer and changes the masked ball to an arena of death. Outside the castle the peasants are dying from the plague, a physical malady, while inside the partygoers are dying from spiritual death of the soul. A mingling of the physical and spiritual are seen in Red Death, whom Prospero takes as a messenger of the devil. Robert Towne's screenplay was the basis for AIP's TOMB OF LIGEIA (1964). Vincent Price is cast as a necrophile turned drug addict and masochistically inclined to be taken over by his wife's spirit. AN EVENING WITH EDGAR ALLEN POE (1973) and SPECTRE OF EDGAR ALLEN POE added to the list of Gothic-inspired horror films.

The anthology film takes a much more restrained if not comic look at human frailities, which Poe saw as evil and horrible. RETURN FROM THE PAST (1967) was an anthology of the supernatural, with Lon Chaney, Jr. as a messenger of the devil who pieced the short stories together. In ILLUSTRATED MAN (1969) Rod Steiger was the main theme linking together a number of short stories. One of the best anthology films, which also established Amicus Productions as a growing company in the field of horror, was DR. TERROR'S HOUSE OF HORRORS (1964), with Peter Cushing as a reader of the Tarot who comes across some businessmen on a train bound unbeknownst to them for death. The victims meet death, as told to them by Cushing's Tarot cards, from man-eating plants, werewolves, vampires, and a voodoo curse. Columbia's TORTURE GARDEN followed in 1968, with Burgess Meridith as a doctor who gathers a group of people together and tells them horror tales about each other. SPIRITS OF THE DEAD (1969) was a Poe-based anthology film. *The Mitzengerstein* was directed by Roger Vadim and starred Jane Fonda as a depraved countess in love with a baron. He rejects her, causing her to murder. *William Wilson* was another Poe tale, directed by Louis Malle and starring Alain Delon and Brigitte Bardot. Wilson has guilt feelings about murder, which causes him to go to confession, where he relates his story. As a child he was a sadist, always the bully.

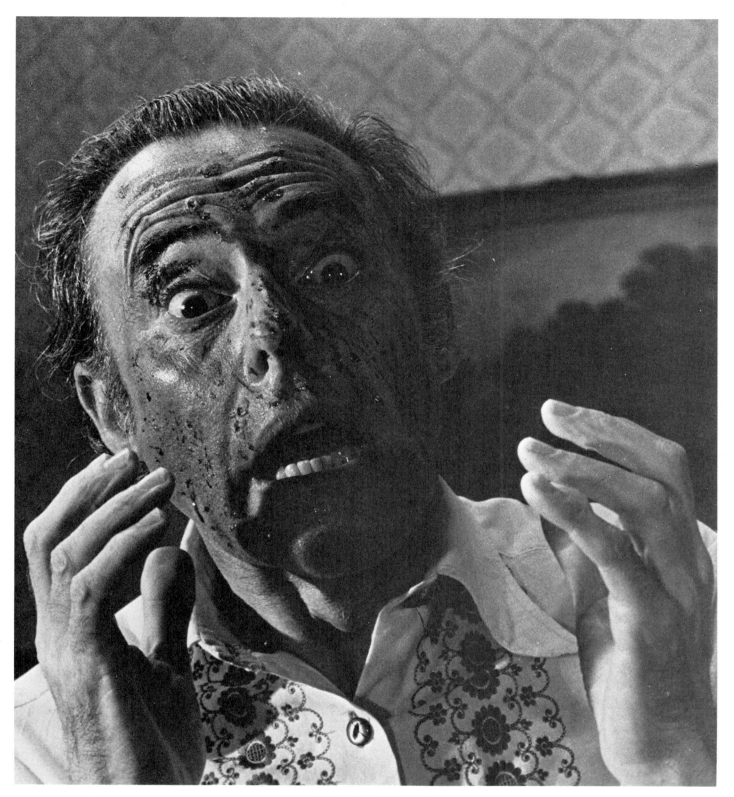

"Vault of Horror"

He goes to medical school, only to revel in drinking and threaten to amputate a girl's breast at a live autopsy procedure. Confession doesn't provide him with the forgiveness he seeks, whereupon he commits suicide. *Tobey Damnit, or Never Bet the Devil Your Head* offered Terence Stamp as a racing driver who picks up a little girl. While driving she dares him to jump the car over a dangerous bridge, which he does, resulting in his decapitation.

ASYLUM (1972) was an Amicus anthology pieced together by a doctor who seeks employment as the head of an asylum. He will get the job if he can pick out the former head, one of a number of patients whom he will see. The patients provide the stories. The film combines the talents of Milt Subotsky and Max Rosenberg, who are responsible for a number of Amicus horror films. Their writing and production work well. TALES FROM THE CRYPT (1971), AND NOW THE SCREAMING STARTS (1973), TALES THAT WITNESS MADNESS, THE HOUSE THAT DRIPPED BLOOD, and VAULT OF HORROR all show the new outlet that the horror film was taking. The latter was a 1973 Amicus film wherein a group of office workers become trapped in the basement, where they await someone to rescue them. Meanwhile, each relates a different horror story to the group. Amicus' FROM BEYOND THE GRAVE (1974) was a four-story anthology film, with Peter Cushing cast as an antique dealer who is swindled by his customers. But each antique carries its own added surprise. A man purchases a mirror for his apartment that encloses a trapped monk. The Rasputin-like image possesses his soul, causing him to procure young girls and slaughter them, providing the image with enough strength to come out of the mirror. Other tales concern an English couple whose domestic bickering causes a child to pray for their death. His prayers are answered by a witch, who brings death to his parents. A businessman's wife is taken over by an evil force. The final tale, perhaps the best, is the longest of the four. A young couple purchases a door, which houses a blue room with an evil centuries-old Englishman, who desires the man's spouse. The man is destroyed when the girl axes a wooden image of him on the door, causing the room to be destroyed. They are spared because the antique dealer discovers that the man didn't cheat him out of the sale or steal his money, as did the not so fortunate clients.

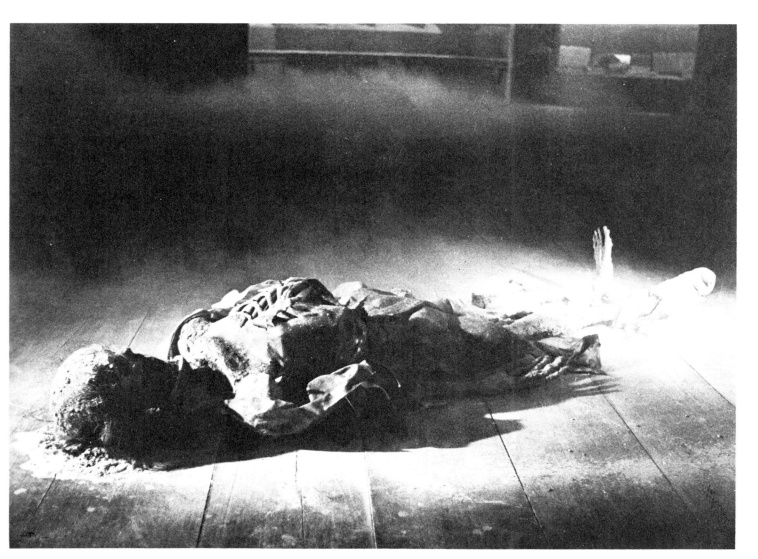

"From Beyond the Grave"

chapter 9

TO EARTH AND BEYOND!

SCIENCE FICTION SPARKS the imagination with fantastic stories based on distortion of established scientific facts. The cinema of the sci-fi thriller is composed of three areas. The first, which accounts for at least 50% of the films, comprises the outer-space-oriented film, which is divided into two categories: the first deals with alien life forms visiting earth, while the second offers humans as alien life forms visiting other worlds. The second type of science-fiction film deals with tales related to ever-increasing technology. Here the horror comes out of the laboratory or from scientific advances that culminate in journeys under the oceans or under the earth's crust. The last area, equally as popular as the outer-space sagas, includes the future-oriented premonition films. Like the first, this area is further divided into two categories. The first declares that our doom will come from final wars and doomsday devices, a nifty idea arising out of the cold-war feeling of the late fifties. Like the doomsday device, this idea died after a few years and became a fad of the past. The second category of the future is just as pessimistic: mankind is doomed to individual destruction by a computer-dominated society with little regard for human emotions. Sci-fi takes the radical point of view. While horror and fantasy tales are based on the past or the present, the sci-fi film ignores it and turns to the future for inspiration.

The differences between the three genres are interesting. While sci-fi is based on a distortion of established fact, both horror and fantasy are not based on reality at all and are therefore more concerned with shocking the viewer's emotions than with sparking his imagination. Interest in sci-fi is motivated by a desire on the part of the avid reader, filmgoer, and buff to believe in the possibilities of other life forms and fantastic technology. This motivation is made possible by the magnificent array of special effects that

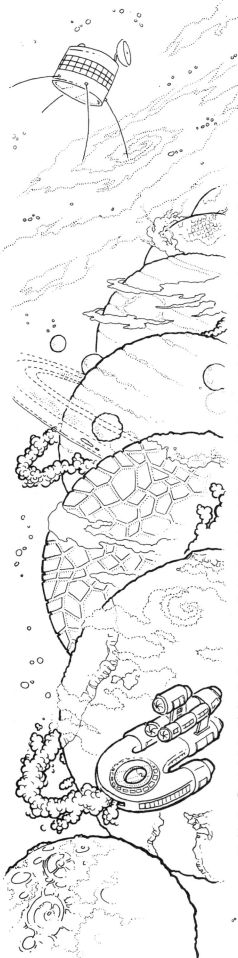

transform our ideas into celluloid reality, and by a good script. From the early beginnings of the sci-fi genre, which inspired such writers as Wells, Verne, Asimov, Heinlein, Bradbury, and others, to the early pulps of the thirties and forties, *Amazing, Astounding, Weird Tales,* and *Fantastic Stories,* to the sophisticated sci-fi sagas of today, belief in the impossible as possible continues to grow and nourish. This chapter describes the first two types of science-fiction film.

Each sci-fi filmmaker envisions his own idea of alien life forms and how they influence us. The idea of extraterrestrial visits isn't all that new when one ponders how long ago H. G. Wells conceived his *War of the Worlds*. The book inspired such films as George Melies' A TRIP TO THE MOON (1902). His concepts of a big bullet-shaped rocket fired from a cannon came from the writings of Jules Verne, while his description of alien life forms comes from Wells' *Selenites*, insectlike creatures with a high degree of intelligence. WHIRLING THE WORLDS (1904), VOYAGE TO A STAR, AROUND A STAR (1906), A TRIP TO JUPITER, A TRIP TO MARS, and VOYAGE TO THE MOON (1909) continued the sci-fi genre. What was sci-fi in the time of Melies and Wells is now established fact, since we have indeed journeyed to the moon.

FIRST MEN IN THE MOON (1919) was remade in 1964 by Columbia Pictures. Fritz Lang's GIRL IN THE MOON and AELITA were also conceived during cinema's discovery of sci-fi. Interest in the genre waned during the thirties, due in part to the interest in screen horror, with the exception of the Flash Gordon and Buck Rogers serials. The late forties and early fifties saw interest in the subject pick up with the sci-fi serial. Republic's THE PURPLE MONSTER STRIKES was a 15-part film directed by Spencer Bennett and Fred Brennan. They envisioned aliens, played by Roy Barcroft in a suit of scales, paving the way for an invasion from Mars. FLYING DISC MEN FROM MARS (1951) were alien gangsters who sought world domination. RADAR MEN FROM THE MOON (1952) introduced the popular government agent Commando Cody, played here by George Wallace. Cody sported a bullet-shaped helmet and black-leather-jacketed rocket suit. Cody returned in THE LOST PLANET and ZOMBIES OF THE STRATOSPHERE (1952). The latter film told of a band of aliens helping an earthman to create an H-bomb to be used to blast the earth out of its orbit so that the alien planet could utilize our atmosphere. George Pal's DESTINATION MOON (1950) for United Artists lacked aliens and monsters and concentrated on technology. ROCKETSHIP XM visited Mars and depicted it as a barren red desert—very true to life! Other low-budget space haunts followed, among them: FLIGHT TO MARS, SPACEWAYS, CAT WOMEN OF THE MOON (aliens depicted as lovelies clad in miniskirts), SATELLITE IN THE SKY (1956), and FIRE MAIDENS FROM OUTER SPACE (more girls clad in short tunics).

"Atragon", a Japanese blend of sci-fi and fantasy

FOX'S THE DAY THE EARTH STOOD STILL (1951) was directed by Robert Wise, who envisioned aliens as soft-spoken and highly intelligent. Michael Rennie's Klaatu, a messenger from outer space, arrives in a spaceship with a message: cease testing nuclear weapons or be destroyed. Gort, a robot companion, is also on hand to carry out Klaatu's threat. THE THING (1951) was produced by Howard Hawks, who envisioned aliens as vegetable men, such as the monster played by James Arness. Directed by Christian Nyby, the plot takes place at a polar army base, where the alien is discovered frozen in a block of ice. The thing thaws out and plays a deadly game of cat-and-mouse, winding up cooked with electricity. The thing had the ability to regenerate its limbs and fed on blood. INVADERS FROM MARS (1952) came from Fox studios and saw Martians as bugeyed invaders that served a green head with a myriad of tentacles encased in a bubble. Victims drop into this underground chamber, only to reappear later with crystals embedded in their necks. Jack Arnold saw the alien as an unseen thing that can inhabit the body of an individual in his IT CAME FROM OUTER SPACE, made the following year for Universal and based on a Ray Bradbury story. KILLERS FROM SPACE, PHANTOM FROM SPACE, DEVIL GIRL FROM MARS (1954), ROBOT MASTER, and STRANGER FROM VENUS were low-budget looks at aliens.

Paramount's WAR OF THE WORLDS, produced by George Pal, was based on an H. G. Wells novel. While lacking any sort of message, the film does provide spectacular special effects of Martian Hovercraft—Manta-ray-shaped spaceships that spew death rays at the army. The Martians themselves are depicted as lurid large orbs, long necks, and arms, ending in three suction-tipped appendages. Universal's THIS ISLAND EARTH (1953) concerned the efforts of two scientists to save an alien world from destruction. Metaluna is at war with Zhagon, and their protective field is crumbling under attack. Also menacing the travelers is a Metalunan—a skull-like face under a large, cerebral, pulsating mass with five insect mouths and lobster-like claws—fashioned equally as horrendously in a series of Mars Attack bubble-gum cards from the late fifties. The creature is matched only by the special effects of the interplanetary war, shown with mattes but nonetheless visually exciting. Hammer's QUARTERMASS series of films, MGM's FORBIDDEN PLANET (1956), where the alien was a manifestation of the subconscious mind, SPACE MONSTER X7, X THE UNKNOWN (1957), QUEEN OF OUTER SPACE, THE BRAIN EATERS, and NIGHT OF THE BLOOD BEAST (1957) from AIP showed aliens as a multitude of beasts and evil personages.

IT! THE TERROR FROM OUTER SPACE was a blood-drinking alien monster, played by Crash Corrigan of UNDERSEA KINGDOM fame. Most of the action occurs aboard a spaceship returning to Earth. The alien is a stow-

"Yog -- Monster From Space"

away who plays a cat-and-mouse game with the crew. Claustrophobia between the thing's advances to the main deck of the ship and the crew's last hold provides the excitement. Claustrophobia was treated in a different way—across the deserted city of Chicago—in Allied Artists' TARGET EARTH. The film shows a Venusian invasion underway, as robots lurk among the desolate city after a group of people try to find a way out to safety. Claustrophobia was also used as a devise in Don Seigel's INVASION OF THE BODY SNATCHERS (1956). Seigel envisioned aliens taking over the bodies of the residents of a small town, Santa Mira. Subtlety also accounts for the film's success. Seed pods turn into exact replicas of residents, and while they sleep, their minds are taken over. Loss of emotion, the ability to feel and give love, is the horror that awaits us. Kevin McCarthy and Dana Winter try to elude the growing number of alien takeovers in the town, fleeing desperately to the next town to relate their tale to the authorities. Other films were less notable, suffering from bad scripts and low budgets: HAVE ROCKET WILL TRAVEL (1959), BATTLE IN OUTER SPACE, MISSILE TO THE MOON, BEAST WITH A MILLION EYES, and THE MONOLITH MONSTERS (1957). The latter film depicted aliens as giant meteorites in the desert.

Man visited other worlds and returned the worse for it in MGM's MAN IN SPACE, where the astronaut turns into a fungoid mass of evil. PHANTOM PLANET (1960) caused visitors to shrink to a minuscule size. 12 TO THE MOON, PLANETS AGAINST US, THREE STOOGES IN ORBIT, VISIT TO A SMALL PLANET, ASSIGNMENT OUTER SPACE (1962), WAR OF THE SATELLITES, COSMIC MAN, INVASION OF THE SAUCERMEN (1959), with aliens depicted by AIP as midgets with oversized heads, THE CAPE CANAVERAL MONSTERS, THE HUMAN DUPLI- CATORS, THE EARTH DIES SCREAMING, and THE DAY MARS INVADED EARTH all offered sci-fi fright fare. AIP's THE ANGRY RED PLANET (1959) was based on a story by Ib Melchoir about a space crew who lands on Mars. The crew encounters a myriad of alien life, such as man-eating plants, a giant bat-rat- spider, and a blob of protoplasm that threatens to devour the ship. The film is also shot in multitones, offering a weird, colorful look at the planet. BRAIN FROM PLANET AROUS (1957) took over the mind of John Agar and exerted evil influence. Gor, the evil brain, was counteracted by Vol, the good brain, which inhabited the body of Agar's pet dog. Columbia's TWENTY MILLION MILES TO EARTH involved an animated alien conjured by Ray Harryhausen as an Ymir, an example of life on Venus, which, due to the earth's atmo- sphere, goes metabolically out of control. The Ymir, a giant creature with the face of a dragon, the body of a two-legged creature, and a serpentine tail, goes on a rampage throughout Italy. I MARRIED A MONSTER FROM OUTER SPACE (1958) featured a glowing creature that planned on intermarrying with

"The Eye Creatures"

earthlings, while INVISIBLE INVADERS (1959) were alien forces who inhabited the dead. Toho's THE MYSTERIANS (1958) also planned on intermarrying with Earth women, while PLAN NINE FROM OUTER SPACE (1956) offered Tor Johnson, Vampira, and Bela Lugosi as a mute.

Columbia's EARTH VS THE FLYING SAUCERS, made in 1957 under the special-effects mastery of Ray Harryhausen, were manned by androids who attacked Washington with ray guns from amazing flying saucers. The many landmarks under saucer attack provide the thrills. AIP's IT CONQUERED THE WORLD (1957) envisioned the alien as a Venusian influencing earthmen into aiding a takeover. The creature is depicted as a giant cucumber monster with giant claws, an evil-looking face, and antennae atop its head. NOT OF THIS EARTH, also made in 1957, offered Paul Birch as Mr. Johnson, a visitor from the planet Davanna looking for new blood on Earth. KRONOS (1957) was a giant robot that fed on atomic energy. UA's DAY OF THE TRIFFIDS 1962 was based on a John Wyndham story about man-eating plants. Another evil alien was Medra a visitor from the planet Ganymede in BLOOD BEAST FROM OUTER SPACE. He was a horribly disfigured man who sought females in ads placed in the local papers for models. THE TERRORNAUTS (1967) and THEY CAME FROM OUTER SPACE took other glimpses of alien life forms.

Sci-fi films in the second category, earthlings journeying to other worlds as aliens, are equally numerous. The astronaut appeared in such fare as BATTLE BEYOND THE SUN (1962), VOYAGE TO THE END OF THE UNIVERSE (1963), MASTERS OF VENUS, BEAST WITH FIVE FINGERS (1964), BATTLE OF THE WORLDS, SPACEWAYS, ROBINSON CRUSOE ON MARS, FIRST MEN IN THE MOON (1964), MUTINY IN OUTER SPACE (1965), WAY WAY OUT (1966), TO THE MOON AND BEYOND, MISSION MARS, and COUNTDOWN. The action no longer took place on the Earth but in some desolate region of the galaxy. Mario Bava's PLANET OF THE VAMPIRES for AIP put the space crew in a world that bred a myriad of hallucinogenic horrors. WOMEN OF THE PREHISTORIC PLANET (1966) and VOYAGE TO A PREHISTORIC PLANET mixed sex and archaic worlds. AIP'S QUEEN OF BLOOD (1966) was Florence Marly, an alien vampire threatening a space crew. JOURNEY TO THE FAR SIDE OF THE SUN (1969) had Roy Thinnes (David Vincent of *Invaders* television fame) as an astronaut returning to what he believes is the earth but is in fact a mirror world of his home planet. Hammer's MOON ZERO TWO (1969) offered James Olsen (ANDROMEDA STRAIN) in a space story that mixed interplanetary technology with an old-west flavor. THE GREEN SLIME (1969) was an out-and-out parody about a space crew that must defend itself and the space station against a fungus attack.

"Battle Beyond the Sun"

The second type of sci-fi film doesn't necessarily take place in the vast, inky blackness of space itself. It can take place under the sea, as evidenced by VOYAGE TO THE BOTTOM OF THE SEA, AROUND THE WORLD UNDER THE SEA, THE NEPTUNE FACTOR, and DESTINATION INNER SPACE (1966). The latter film shows an undersea colony under attack by outer-space creatures from a submerged spacecraft, blending outer space and inner space, as did THE ATOMIC SUBMARINE, wherein a creature played havoc with the Navy. JOURNEY TO THE CENTER OF THE EARTH, and AT THE EARTH'S CORE (1976) combine the imagination of the fantasy film with the gimmicky scientific apparatus of the sci-fi thriller.

Stanley Kubrick's 2001: A SPACE ODYSSEY was based on Arthur C. Clarke's novel. Astronauts find themselves on a lunar base and at wits against an evil computer, Hal. The main theme goes deeper: intellect developing in primates is shown by a primitive weapon changing into a space ship. The increase in science and technology culminates in 2001 A. D. when man has achieved all he can and a star child, shown as an embryo floating in space, is the symbol for a new civilization. The brilliant and sophisticated special effects outshine anything done before. MAROONED (1970) was taken from a real-life incident: an Apollo crew is helpless and in trouble in space. SILENT RUNNING (1971) was Douglas Trumball's entry into the field of sci-fi. Here Bruce Dern and fellow astronauts are on a space station that holds the last bit of greenery on the earth. There is an order to destroy it, and Dern goes berserk, doing anything he can, including murder, to save the flora. Special effects make the film attractive. SOLARIS and FANTASTIC PLANET (1974) follow the style of the sci-fi-oriented film. The latter is a full-length cartoon.

THE ANDROMEDA STRAIN based on Michael Crichton's novel, poses the question as to what could happen if an unmanned spacecraft returns with a deadly germ that could wipe out all life on earth. Pierre Boule's novel *The Monkey Planet* gave a new life to the astronaut-oriented film as Twentieth Century Fox's PLANET OF THE APES (1968).

The plot describes a space crew, led by Charleton Heston as Taylor, landing on a planet ruled by a culture of apes. The simian culture sees humans as slaves and imprisons them for research. The entire culture is ape-ruled, but Taylor is befriended by a pair of benevolent researchers, Zira (Kim Hunter) and Cornelius (Roddy McDowell). Taylor escapes to the Forbidden Zone, chased by armies of gorillas, only to discover the relic of a past world, the Statue of Liberty, on a beach, telling Taylor the horrible truth—the Planet of the Apes is the Earth! BENEATH THE PLANET OF THE APES (1970) had another astronaut trying to rescue Taylor but also discover-

The phallic spaceship in "Flesh Gordon"

ing the inevitable. The film offers ruins of the Stock Exchange, an abandoned railroad station, and the Radio City Music Hall. Radioactive mutations who live underground and worship the power of the bomb are caught up in a battle between themselves and the apes, which results in the destruction of the world. ESCAPE FROM THE PLANET OF THE APES (1971) shows Zira and Cornelius escaping in a space capsule in a time warp prior to the explosion and landing on Earth many years hence, where they are captured by society and put on exhibition as freaks. Realizing that their lives are in danger, they flee, only to die. Before Zira dies she gives birth to a child, Milo. In CONQUEST OF THE PLANET OF THE APES (1974) Milo is grown up, a slave in a society that breeds apes as slave labor to do menial tasks. Milo, now called Caesar, revolts and starts a counterrevolution against the humans with an army of fellow slaves. The well-made and very successful series culminated in BATTLE FOR THE PLANET OF THE APES (1975).

The astronaut's exploits were parodied by two filmmakers, Jean Claude Forest, in his comic-strip heroine BARBARELLA, played camply by Jane Fonda, and Mammoth's FLESH GORDON (1975). Roger Vadim directed Jane Fonda as Barbarella, an outer-space heroine whose exploits on a pop-art planet cause her to meet a blind angel, demon dolls, tree people, rock people, an evil queen, outer-space gimmickry and an evil machine that she wears out with her orgasms. FLESH GORDON is a sex-oriented satire on the original thirties film starring Buster Crabbe. The planet Mongo is Porno; Dale Arden is Dale Ardor, who flaunts her lovely bosom throughout the film; Dr. Zarkov is Dr. Flexi Jerkoff, who is a dead ringer for Frank Shannon's character, Ming is cast as Wang the Perverted, who looks like a transvestite. The planet Porno is bombarding the Earth with sex rays that cause world-wide orgies. Flesh and his friends blast off in a phallic-shaped rocket ship to the planet Porno and encounter breasty vampire women, raping robots with cork-screw screwers, a swordfighting insect, a giant penisaurus who goes after Dale, a lesbian queen with an eyepatch, a queen armed with power pasties that emit laser beams, and, a parody on the old King Kong original, a giant ogre who seizes Dale and carries her to the top of Wang's phallic-shaped palace, where he comments on the size of her breasts as Flesh drives the space ship up his rear end! The film is a colorful rehash of the original whose success is due in part to the animation of Tom Sherman and Robert Maine. The film was produced and directed by Howard Ziehm.

chapter 10

FUTURE SHOCK

AND DESTRUCTION

ONE AREA OF SCIENCE FICTION that never ceases to create a stir is Premonition. The dictionary defines it as forewarning. This style of science fiction grew out of the fifties' ever-increasing technology in atomic and nuclear physics. Premonitions of a future society or of nuclear destruction are found in many science-fiction films, which are divided into two types: the first deals with the pessimistic attitude that our own inability to share the earth with other races of peoples plus an increasing scale of weapons will be the basis for our future destruction; the second explores the concept of destruction in the future because of humanistic reasons—a society that is overpopulated, underfed, and, most importantly, undermined by computerism, disregard for individualism, lack of love, and inability to express human emotions. Human emotions are seen as a menace to the concept of totalitarianism. In either case pessimism provides the impetus for the ensuing conflicts and action.

According to the first viewpoint we will never reach the future: our devastation will come now. The turmoil arises out of final wars and dangerous experiments with the power of the atom. The cycle of havoc films began in 1910. As scientific technology was largely unknown, the end came from outer space, as in THE COMET and COMET'S COMEBACK (1916). END OF THE WORLD (1931) came from tidal waves and earthquakes. This formula was a blueprint for seventies disaster films. The fifties inspired the idea of a final war: This popular concept arose from the state of affairs between Russia and the U.S.A., each regarding the other as spy-oriented and subversive. Other related reasons were the Cold War, the Gary Powers incident, the rise of McCarthyism, which further instilled the horrors of Communism in the hearts of the American people, and an ever-increasing weaponry, supported by the arms race. This wave of paronoia inspired some people to

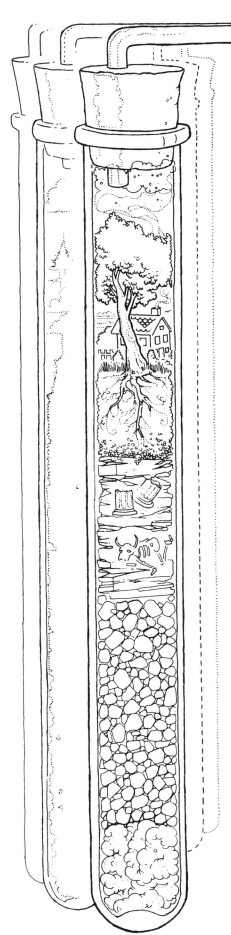

spend their money on bomb shelters. The private-school and public-school systems to this day practice air raids.

As if deluge wasn't bad enough, FIVE (1951) told the story of the final five survivors of a nuclear war. CAPTIVE WOMEN (1952) was set in the year 3000 and involved a race of Amazons fighting for their virginity against horrible radioactive-contaminated mutants. INVASION USA, (1953) also followed the boom of destruction. These films were a far cry from the destruction of a small group of people, as in Paramount's DR. CYCLOPS with Albert Dekker, the 1940s answer to world destruction. George Pal's WHEN WORLDS COLLIDE (1951) was Paramount's answer to world devastation. The planet Bellus is on a collision course with earth, and a select 40 hurried to safety to start a new world on the planet Zyra. THE DAY THE WORLD ENDED (1955) was a low-budget film by Roger Corman, which nevertheless set the tone of future movies. The world has already been destroyed by nuclear warfare, and a handful of survivors hold up in a mountain cabin. The group mimics a sprinkling of types, from the good, seen in Richard Carlson and Lori Nelson, who typify the new Adam and Eve, to Mike Connors, a gangster, his stripper girlfriend, and a beggar, symbolic of the bad. Paul Blaisdell is a mutant whose efforts in carrying off Lori Nelson threaten the birth of that new world. Corman's film is the best fifties film on the subject, and despite the poor budget it carries impact. Earth's destruction came from many different causes, as shown by THE NIGHT THE WORLD EXPLODED (1957), in which an element in the Carlsbad Caverns was responsible for the trouble. The effects of a final war were shown in THE LAST WOMAN ON EARTH (1960), THE WORLD THE FLESH AND THE DEVIL, ROCKET ATTACK USA (1961), THE FINAL WAR, THE LOST MISSILE, and ON THE BEACH.

Radiation's effects on man were explored in Jack Arnold's THE INCREDIBLE SHRINKING MAN (1957) for Universal. The hero, Grant Williams, shrinks after his exposure and is menaced by his pet cat, now a monster, and a spider. He stays alive long enough to reach a window. The camera shows Williams looking out through the screen holes, each camera glimpse getting larger until the camera pans out into space. That final moment, a film classic in itself, shows the increasing smallness of the hero until he vanishes into another world. Similar exercises in the horror of smallness were shown in AIP's ATTACK OF THE PUPPET PEOPLE (1958). Other effects of radiation caused different-sized problems, such as Col. Glenn Manning, who grew into THE AMAZING COLOSSAL MAN (1957) as a result of a plutonium blast. So successful was the film that it inspired a sequel, WAR OF THE COLOSSAL BEAST. The female was not overlooked, as evidenced by Allison Hayes' ATTACK OF THE FIFTY FOOT WOMAN and Dorothy Provine as THE THIRTY FOOT BRIDE OF CANDY ROCK.

Nuclear warfare was also the subject of some tense dramas, such as FAILSAFE, DR. STRANGELOVE, and THE DAY THE FISH CAME OUT. DAY THE

"Monster From a Prehistoric Planet"

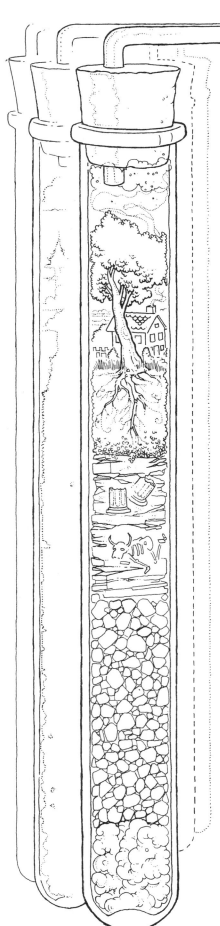

EARTH CAUGHT FIRE (1961) was caused by two atomic blasts occurring at both poles, which resulted in a shift of the Earth's axis. Directed by Val Guest, the film's low budget never allowed it to live up to the title. AIP's PANIC IN THE YEAR ZERO (1962) showed a family's plight to stay alive after an atomic war. THE DAY THE EARTH FROZE (1963) was the result of a witch's hex. Excelsior's THE DAY THE SKY EXPLODED (1961) had a missile exploding and burning up the sky. Dana Andrews' efforts to reach the core of the Earth were shown in CRACK IN THE WORLD (1965). MGM's BATTLE BENEATH THE EARTH (1968) had a warlord waging war on the USA underground. AIP's WILD IN THE STREETS (1968) cast Christopher Jones as a rock singer elected President, who starts concentration camps for all over thirty, but a third generation is starting to think that twenty-five is awfully old.

Many versions of Richard Matheson's *I Am Legend* appeared in cinema, starting with Vincent Price in AIP's THE LAST MAN ON EARTH (1964). Warner's THE OMEGA MAN (1971) cast Charlton Heston as the hero who runs amok in California after a nuclear holocaust and fights off mutant vampires and contamination. This idea also occurs in George Romero's NIGHT OF THE LIVING DEAD (1968), which became a cult film. For some inexplicable reason the dead arise and seek the living for food. Ben and a handful of survivors hole up in a deserted house and fight off the newly risen dead, but they don't last long. The corpses rip out innards and devour them greedily. At the end Ben is mistaken for one of the dead, shot in the head, and placed on a pile of corpses and incinerated by authorities when the national disaster is declared over. Columbia's CHOSEN SURVIVORS (1974) were sent underground after a nuclear war, where they live out their existences until a group of vampire bats attacks. Later we are told that the idea was merely a hoax, an experiment by the government to check the effects of confinement in the event of the real thing.

These films are comparable to other areas of the cinema of the bizarre in giving the viewer a genuine fright. What is shown did and could possibly happen to anyone. Therein lies the horror impact. The box-office success of these films made filmmakers turn to similar perils. Since the idea of a nuclear war had become unpopular and (hopefully) unrealistic, the new films were content to show airplane crashes, floods, quakes, and burning buildings. The destruction seen previously as affecting an entire populace was now confined to a small group. The special effects, on the other hand, were more elaborate than previous disaster films. Top-notch producers and filmmakers joined big-budgeted companies to offer filmgoers some frightening fare. THE POSEIDON ADVENTURE and VOLCANO were the first in a wave of disasters to come. AIRPORT inspired a sequel, AIRPORT '75. Of the disaster films the worst was TIDAL WAVE (1975), about the submergence of Japan. The best films on the subject come from the United States. THE TOWERING INFERNO (1975), from Warner's and Fox, is a masterpiece of special effects

"The Crazies"

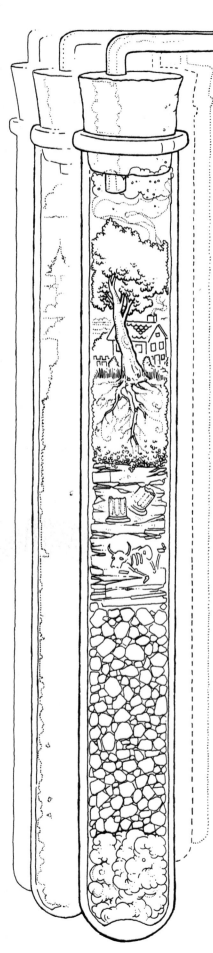

and excitement. The second-best film is EARTHQUAKE (1975), from Universal, which introduced the added surprise of Sensurround. INFERNO, based on two best sellers and adapted for the screenplay by Stirling Silliphant, tells the story of a giant superstructure that catches fire, trapping people inside. Since the structure is so tall, it is difficult for the fire department to rescue the people. The film provides both a warning to builders and a memorial to firemen. Irwin Allen's special effects, along with a big cast, make the film succeed. EARTHQUAKE, on the other hand, shows the devastation caused by a giant tremor that rips apart Los Angeles. The effects won numerous Academy Awards. Sensurround is a sound system that engulfs the audience in a sea of vibrations similar to what one would experience in a quake. The vibrations are produced on a separate soundtrack and played out of giant speakers surrounding the theater.

The second type of the science-fiction destruction presents mankind in the future. The pessimism is shown through absorbing screenplays. Sci-fi writers presented the future through a valley of gloom: overpopulation, starvation, ever-increasing technology, biological mutations, and the Orwellian concept of totalitarianism are the areas most in vogue.

The idea isn't new, as evidenced by Fritz Lang's METROPOLIS, made in 1928. The film offers Lang's statement on the future. Society will be run by a vast, monsterlike system of machines and will be served by laborers who are almost slaves. The factories are owned by the rich upper class but operated by a poverty-stricken lower class that lives out its existence like rats, living beneath the machines it serves. The year is 2000 AD. The film shows a man called Fredersen aiding his brothers, who live underground, in a revolt against the rich. Lang's view of the future most likely grew out of his surroundings in postwar Berlin. A girl, Maria, represents the pacifist attitude towards a revolt. Rotwang, played by Rudolph Klein Rogge, is the leader of the rich class. He creates a robotlike image of Maria to spur the workers into revolution. In destroying the monstrous labyrinth of machines the workers have unsuspectedly drowned their homes and families, who live underground. Upon realizing this they turn on the Robotrix, and Maria and Fredersen act in time to save the children from the floods. Although outdated, the film's special effects and sets are quite good for the era, especially when one of the machines is changed into a leering face of a devil. Lang's tale shows how the modern metropolis and increasing technology threaten the existence of the family unit as well as the freedom of the individual.

Equally as thrilling in special effects depicting a modern world of the future but lacking the quality of a good screenplay were JUST IMAGINE and THE TUNNEL. Miniatures were constructed to depict the large, omniscient city of the future. THE SHAPE OF THINGS TO COME (1936) was a United Artists release based on an H.G. Wells story. The film takes place in Everytown in

Maria cries for help in "Metropolis"

the year 1970 at the end of a final war. By 2036 peace is finally realized, but space travel, which represents the new technology, is threatened by the efforts of a band of saboteurs. Sets are quite elaborate and futuristically constructed. The future has little regard for man's individuality, as evidenced by both the story and film of George Orwell's 1984, made by Associated British in 1955. The film's plot deals with a man's daring in loving a fellow human being. The couple fights back at Big Brother's authoritarian state. Totalitarianism is indeed a Nazilike dogma, relating to a political regime based on subordination of the individual to the strict control of the state in all aspects of life. Individual morality is likened by the state to cancer.

Allied Artists' WORLD WITHOUT END (1956) envisioned an even gloomier world. A crew on their way to Mars hit a time barrier, which caused them to land in the future on a desolate war-ravaged planet that they grimly realize is Earth! Radioactive mutations formed from the fallout of nuclear warfare inhabit the surface of the planet, living in caves as barbarians while civilized and intelligent humans live beneath the surface in a labyrinth of constructed buildings. This race is stagnated due to the lack of children. The space crew, after meeting with memories of their own families who grew old and died, become the saviors of the human race and try to bridge the gap between the two cultures. After a confrontation between the captain of the crew and the leader of the barbarians the two cultures slowly become one. The climax shows barbarian children and civilized children playing and learning together among a group of buildings crudely being constructed in the background.

Some silly films were made on the subject in a weak attempt to cash in on big money. Among the low-budget offerings were MAN FROM 1997 (1957), TERROR IN THE YEAR 5000 (1958), ATOMIC MAN (1963), THE TIME TRAVELLERS, written and directed by Ib Melchoir, and a number of robot-oriented films, such as DR. WHO AND THE DALEKS, CREATION OF THE HUMANOIDS, DALEKS INVASION EARTH 2150 A.D., IN THE YEAR 2885 (1968), wherein a group of people hole up in a cave after a final war leaves a horrible mutation that kills survivors, and DEATH RACE 2000 (1975). The latter film shows a car race of the future in which pedestrians are killed by cars in an effort to rack up points by drivers. ATLANTIS THE LOST CONTINENT (1961), SHE (1964), and VENGEANCE OF SHE (1967) all had unusual futuristic sets in which tales of lost civilizations are unearthed. American International's AT THE EARTH'S CORE (1976) was based on Edgar Rice Burroughs' tales of Pelucidar, an underground land at the core of the earth. It includes barbaric civilizations of Mahars, bird women who eat human flesh, Sagoths, animal-faced soldiers, Mosops, animals whose fiery breath can wither trees, and another lovely seductress, Dia, played by Caroline Munro.

Another writer to depict future horrors was H.G. Wells, whose expert

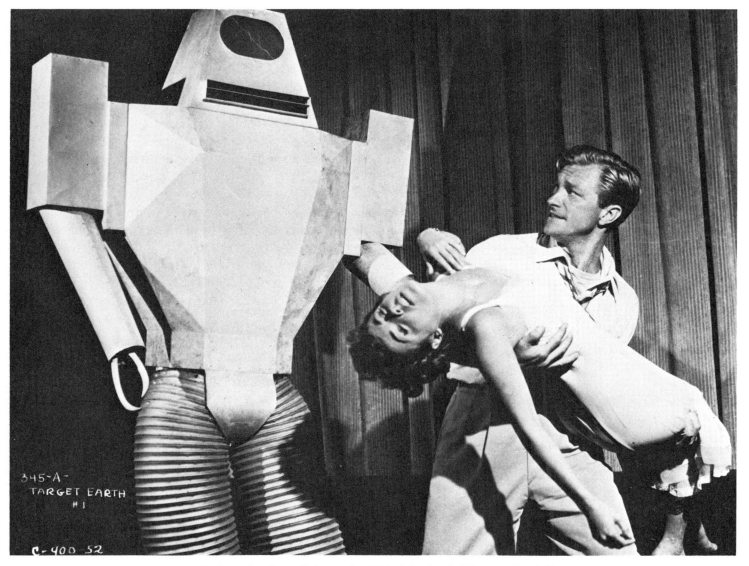

Robots besiege Chicago in Allied Artists' "Target Earth"

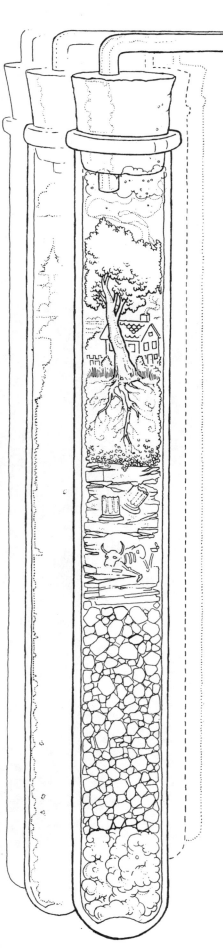

THE TIME MACHINE was brought to the cinema by Pal for MGM in 1960. Rod Taylor is George, who, with the aid of a time machine, teleports himself out of the nineteenth century into the future, passing through three world wars, the last in 1966. The planet is scorched and volcanolike. Lava from a volcano threatens to engulf the machine, so George blasts ahead into the year 802,701 A.D. Here history is seen repeating itself. The Eloi are fairhaired, benevolent people who are slaves to the mutant Morlocks. George acts on the Eloi's behalf and tries to free the people from the slavery of the Morlocks. Bill Tuttle's makeup makes the appearance of the Morlocks more comical than horrifying, with their hooflike legs, long, flowing white hair, cross-eyes, and buck teeth. Nevertheless, the idea of repressed benevolence dominated by evil is very entertaining.

Godard's ALPHAVILLE (1965) is another violent and totalitarian vision of the future. Alphaville is a city of the future, and its inhabitants are governed by a giant computer called Alpha 60. The computer takes over people's lives, turning them into zombielike slaves whose only wish is to serve and please. Individual thinking as well as emotions are supressed. Enter hero Lemmy Caution (Eddie Constantine) to investigate the mysterious goings-on. The people are zombielike in their speech patterns and gazing eyes, almost as if they were drugged. The women seem to be programmed only for sex and pleasure. Ray Bradbury's novel was the basis for FARENHEIT 451 a 1966 film by Universal. Oscar Werner is cast as Montag, a fireman whose sole job is to burn down literature seen as subversive by the government. Director François Truffaut gives the viewer a nightmarish view of a future government that suppresses individual thinking and learning and makes people computer-programmed cards. The people's minds are mere cogs in a wheel, mere circuits in a machine that desires to serve the ultimate computer of totalitarianism. Montag falls in love with a subversive reader, played by Julie Christie.

Avco Embassy painted an interesting picture of the future in THE TENTH VICTIM (1966), a campy pop-art look into legalized murder for profit. War is abolished and a private citizen's social and economic status is determined by a government-sponsored game called The Big Hunt. When you slay your tenth victim on television, you acquire riches, power, and fame. The two contestants are both adept at killing. Ursula Andress is shown in the opening sequence killing her ninth victim with a loaded bra. Marcello Mastroianni is her tenth victim, whom she falls in love with. Warner's THX-1138 (1971) also used the formula of a couple daring to find love in a future mechanized society. Kurt Vonnegut's Billy Pilgrim character materialized onto celluloid in SLAUGHTERHOUSE FIVE (1972). Warner's 1973 look at the future was based on an Anthony Burgess novel, A CLOCKWORK ORANGE. In this future setting Alex (Malcom McDowell) is a juvenile delinquent who, with his band of droogs, who wear bowler hats and elaborate makeup, commit all sorts of crimes from murder to rape. Alex is rehabilitated, but the process removes his individuality and will. MGM's SOYLENT GREEN (1973) saw future society as overpopulated, underfed, and drastically polluted. Shortages of food make people eat a processed substance called soylent, which is revealed to be protein-enriched people! Charlton Heston plays the detective who solves the case.

MGM again looked at the future in WESTWORLD (1973). The film showed a vacationing couple, played by Richard Benjamin and James Brolin, who go to a futuristic amusement park called Delos. In Delos you can visit periods of earth history from Roman times to the old West. Our heroes pick the West. Saloon girls are programmed for sex, and the boys play HIGH NOON with android gunslingers. Yul Brynner plays a gunslinger patterned after his role in THE MAGNIFICENT SEVEN. He is an android and keeps coming back for the kill. The sequel, FUTUREWORLD (1976), starred Peter Fonda and Blythe Danner. Robots are programmed specifically for sex and can vacation on Mars for skiing, but again one can't tell the humans from the androids.

John Boorman's ZARDOZ (1974) and Norman Jewison's ROLLERBALL (1975) both take frightening looks at the future. In ZARDOZ Sean Connery plays Zed, a product of the future where society is dominated by violence and barbarians. The violence is directed at people who dare to have children. Violence is directed at sports in Jewison's film, where James Caan stars as a rollerball champ. The game is a mixture of ice hockey, motorcycles, and brass knuckles, a violent game made possible by big-business conglomerates that also rule the world of the future. MGM's LOGAN'S RUN (1976), produced by Saul David, takes another frightening look at the future. In the twenty-third century life exists for pure pleasure, with all the sex and mind trips one could possibly want. All is serene and beautiful in the bubble-topped city until one reaches his thirtieth birthday. All inhabitants are marked by birth with a life flower, which glows bright red until thirty, when it turns black, marking the wearer for death. A computer decides who shall be granted life renewal or death. Logan is a DS man, one who tracks down runners who don't bravely turn themselves in to the computer. Michael York as Logan and his girl, played by Jenny Augutter, run for their lives. The film has a magnificent array of special effects and miniature sets depicting the city, but the plot has been done before and the performances are automated.

The future is presented as a grim place to live. Most of the problems arise not out of a rapidly growing technology but out of society's desire to emulate the excellent performance of the machines. Most sci-fi directors have shown this theme in their films. From Lang's METROPOLIS to LOGAN'S RUN, individuality is looked upon as irresponsible and subversive. This threat, along with the death of emotions, provides the basis for future tales.

chapter 11

MAGICAL JOURNEYS

VIA CELLULOID

FANTASY NEITHER SHOCKS, as does horror, nor distorts scientific fact, as does sci-fi. Fantasy shapes and brings life to our imaginations. This simulation of mental imagery on screen by animation and special effects provides fantasy with its impetus and popularity. Since our imaginations are shaped by our surroundings and past experiences with striking situations, they are mere extensions of the real world and are not impossible. Déjà vu is a feeling that what we are presently involved in has occurred previously—an eerie phenomenon that bridges the gap between real and unreal. The fantasies of our dreams can be played out in reality. The cinema of fantasy takes us inside our imaginations through camera trickery and special effects. The surrealistic scenarios can be devoid of any plausibility.

Fantasy differs from other genres of bizarre cinema in that, while horror and sci-fi are based on a modicum of reality, fantasy works best by divorcing itself from reality and relying on lack of plausibility. Fantasy is not as limited in scope as are the other genres: it can encompass tales related to mythology, legends, adventures of past periods; it can be musical or sexual in nature. The genre relaxes one's mind by taking the viewer on a vacation to places he isn't likely to visit or situations he isn't likely to find himself in. The young are mesmerized by its animation, as are adults, who find the imagery of monsters, both mythological and imagined, one of the

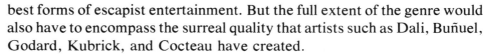

best forms of escapist entertainment. But the full extent of the genre would also have to encompass the surreal quality that artists such as Dali, Buñuel, Godard, Kubrick, and Cocteau have created.

Fantasy has indeed become popular because of its vivid imagery, fantastic sets, and special effects, all used effectively to immerse the viewer in a magical setting removed from reality. Its diverse forms owe their existence to the field of literature. Like horror movies, literature has provided the stories for most fantasy films. Greek tragedies, Homeric epics, the Iliad, the Odyssey, Germanic tales of Siegfried, Viking tales, Norse gods, Roman mythology, Gilgamesh, and knight tales have stimulated fantasy cinema. THE THIEF OF BAGDAD (1927) showed Douglas Fairbanks, Sr., riding over Bagdad on a magic carpet; years later Bergman imprinted the fantasy of death on his SEVENTH SEAL. Cartoons are a good example of the medium. Disney's CINDERELLA, SNOW WHITE, and PINOCCHIO (1939) all derive from famous fairytales written ages ago. George Melies is credited with being the father of fantasy. He perfected the medium by introducing the art of special effects. He contributed to the genre with his CINDERELLA (1899), FANTASTICAL AIRSHIP (1906), CONQUEST OF THE POLE (1912), DIVERS AT WORK ON THE MAINE (1898), and 20,000 LEAGUES UNDER THE SEA.

Fantasy offers escape and states that man's desires and physical wants at times are unattainable, that unreal goals place them in magical or alien surroundings. This is best seen in THE ANDALUSIAN DOG (1929), a collaboration between Salvador Dali and Luis Buñuel. In the film a woman's eye is cut in two with a razor while she sits serene (a statement on man's inhumanity to man and indifference to physical abuse), ants crawl in a hand (symbolic of itching for power or money), and a pair of hands fondle a woman's breasts over her chemise, which vanishes (sexual domination over the will, with moral breakdown the result of physical contact). All are shown as unreal and undesirable goals. Similar in theme is THE AGE OF GOLD. Cocteau's BLOOD OF A POET uses negative imagery, showing the power of the artist in overcoming sex and death. The film is as beautiful as his poetic BEAUTY AND THE BEAST (1945.)

While Alex Korda took us into the lands of the Arabian Nights with THIEF OF BAGDAD (1940), Republic took us into a different fantasy with UNDERSEA KINGDOM (1936), with Ray "Crash" Corrigan and Monte Blue. Disney's fantasy trips are very diverse, from the magical FANTASIA to his

"The Mad Doctor of Blood Island"

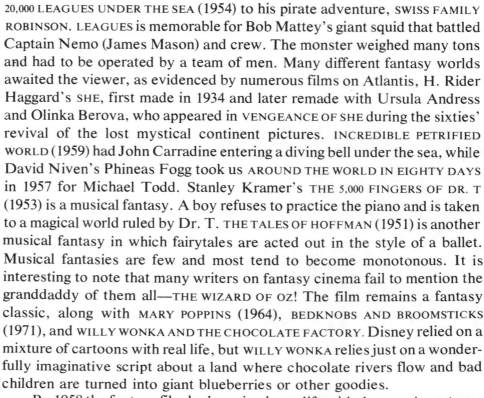

20,000 LEAGUES UNDER THE SEA (1954) to his pirate adventure, SWISS FAMILY ROBINSON. LEAGUES is memorable for Bob Mattey's giant squid that battled Captain Nemo (James Mason) and crew. The monster weighed many tons and had to be operated by a team of men. Many different fantasy worlds awaited the viewer, as evidenced by numerous films on Atlantis, H. Rider Haggard's SHE, first made in 1934 and later remade with Ursula Andress and Olinka Berova, who appeared in VENGEANCE OF SHE during the sixties' revival of the lost mystical continent pictures. INCREDIBLE PETRIFIED WORLD (1959) had John Carradine entering a diving bell under the sea, while David Niven's Phineas Fogg took us AROUND THE WORLD IN EIGHTY DAYS in 1957 for Michael Todd. Stanley Kramer's THE 5,000 FINGERS OF DR. T (1953) is a musical fantasy. A boy refuses to practice the piano and is taken to a magical world ruled by Dr. T. THE TALES OF HOFFMAN (1951) is another musical fantasy in which fairytales are acted out in the style of a ballet. Musical fantasies are few and most tend to become monotonous. It is interesting to note that many writers on fantasy cinema fail to mention the granddaddy of them all—THE WIZARD OF OZ! The film remains a fantasy classic, along with MARY POPPINS (1964), BEDKNOBS AND BROOMSTICKS (1971), and WILLY WONKA AND THE CHOCOLATE FACTORY. Disney relied on a mixture of cartoons with real life, but WILLY WONKA relies just on a wonderfully imaginative script about a land where chocolate rivers flow and bad children are turned into giant blueberries or other goodies.

By 1958 the fantasy film had received new life with the creative talents of Ray Harryhausen, who became known as the king of the animators. His work truly popularized this genre and started a cycle of period fantasy films with Arabian Nights spice. Columbia's SEVENTH VOYAGE OF SINBAD with Kerwin Mathews became the sleeper of the year. Filmed in a process called Dynamation, a term coined by Harryhausen to distinguish his style of animation from others, the film was an absolute success, relying on a myriad of monsters drawn from various mythological tales. The film sported an evil wizard, a cyclops, a dragon, two-headed roc, and a sword-wielding skeleton. THREE WORLDS OF GULLIVER followed, also from Columbia, based on Jonathan Swift's hero. This 1960 film depended mostly on a contrast in size than animation. The effect was achieved with oversized props and shot with split screens and traveling mattes—in other words, different pieces were combined to provide the action in each frame. By this time the process was referred to as SuperDynamation. MGM's THE WONDERFUL WORLD OF THE BROTHERS GRIMM (1962) was a George Pal treat filmed in Cinerama. His SEVEN FACES OF DR. LAO followed. United Artists' MAGIC SWORD was a Bert Gordon fantasy trip based loosely on the legend of Saint George and the dragon. The story is infused with a Vampira, pointy-headed dwarfs and elves, ghouls, and a dragon. Other worlds of fantasy emerging in films at the time were: Columbia's sequel to Verne's LEAGUES, MYSTERIOUS ISLAND, JOURNEY TO THE CENTER OF THE EARTH (1959), JOURNEY BENEATH THE DESERT (1961), and JOURNEY TO THE BEGINNING OF TIME (1966).

Columbia turned to Greece for the mythology of their 1963 film JASON AND THE ARGONAUTS, filmed in color and Dynamation. Harryhausen again amazes us with vivid monsters—winged harpies, king of the sea, a seven-headed hydra of Hades, and the sword-fighting skeleton again, this time with an army that does battle with Jason's crew atop a cliff. The best moment comes when the crew discover a bronzed God, Talos, filled with life by Harryhausen. The first moments of life, when you hear the creaking of bronze and squeaking of the joints, is truly frightening. United Artists' JACK THE GIANT KILLER (1962) brought together Kerwin Mathews and Thorin Thatcher of Sinbad fame, again as archenemies. Jack encounters a room of sword-slashing arms, a two-headed giant, and other magical monsters made possible by George Pal.

There have been many fantasy films about underwater exploits of submarine crews, but none matched the Proteus in Fox' FANTASTIC VOYAGE (1966). The crew of the sub is shrunk and injected into a dying man's arm in a lifesaving operation. The shrinking is done by combining a series of traveling mattes. We are treated to a trip inside the human body through its varied systems. The set constructions for the various systems are quite remarkable, the true stars of the film. Since the sub must travel through fluid, the process was accomplished by filming at high-speed, giving the illusion of water! The film naturally won Academy Awards for its effects.

Columbia's THE VALLEY OF GWANGI, made in 1968, combined dinosaurs with cowboys via the special animation of Mr. Harryhausen. The film is disappointing and is made worse by a love triangle between the stars, but fortunately Gwangi arrives on the screen none to soon. THE GOLDEN VOYAGE OF SINBAD (1974) was the best of this type, made by Columbia and

Ray Harryhausen. The film draws on East Indian legends and myths for its flavor, seen in the goddess Kali—a multiarmed sword wielding statue come to life—a homunculus, a winged griffon, and a centaur. Sinbad was played by John Philip Law (the blind angel of BARBARELLA fame), who gave the role more believeability with his macho image than did the boyish Mathews. Harryhausen's process of animation here was called Dynarama.

Fantasy can even examine the relationships between a man and a woman. These fantasies are seen in a number of films on the human condition. Every man's fantasy of total obsession with a woman was depicted in THE BLUE ANGEL (1930) with Marlene Dietrich in her first and most famous role, Lola. Josef Von Sternberg's direction shows how Lola, the embodiment of true lust, destroys her admirer, a professor (Emil Jannings). His change of role from professor to the clown Pagliacci before an audience of his students and fellow teachers is degrading. He is pelted with eggs while Lola brings about another domination on a strongman in the wings. The professor goes crazy, and his obsession with Lola gives him a heart attack. He dies at his desk in an empty classroom. ECSTASY (1933) had Hedy Lamarr cavorting naked in the forest in a fantasy of elusiveness and orgasm. Federico Fellini depicts relationships as destructive in his films, from LA STRADA (1954) to LA DOLCE VITA (1960) and more recently SATYRICON. Men's fantasies with well-endowed females provided the success of Russ Meyer's films, among them SUPERVIXENS (1975). Sadism is also touched on in a brutal attack on a bitchy girl who demeans a man's libido. The girl is stabbed, drowned, and stomped upon in a tub, after which she emerges from the blood-red waters only to be electrocuted with a radio thrown in for good measure. Sadomasochism was also touched on in BELLE DE JOUR and TRISTANA. Catherine Deneuve is a bored woman who fantasizes about being raped and tortured in her dreams. STORY OF O (1976) and STORY OF JOANNA also regale in sadomaso fantasies. BEHIND THE GREEN DOOR (1975), DEEP THROAT and DEVIL IN MISS JONES put every aspect of sexuality in fantasyland, be it Hades or a mysterious locked room.

The cinema of fantasy encompasses many areas. Perhaps the basic ingredient in a fantasy brew is the total absorption of one's mind in screen goings-on far removed from reality. Without a doubt, be it animation of monsters (most popular) or symbolism cinema, fantasy will continue to enthrall the imagination of its audiences for ages to come.

chapter 12

DIABOLISM

IN FANTASY CINEMA

WHEN ONE THINKS in terms of fantasy, one thinks of magic. Mix this with horror overtones and you have the black magic found in films on diabolism. Witchcraft and devil worship are the most allegorical and at the same time the most censored. Allegory is an expression through symbolic figures and actions of truths or generalizations about human conduct and experience. Censorship goes arm in arm with truism. Throughout history deviltry was suppressed by Puritanism, Romanticism, and the Holy Inquisition, while witchcraft was repressed by Puritan society, the pilgrims, the Church, and the clergy as debauched and unholy. The fact that the two subjects have become taboo is the reason for their popularity. The magical quality of secret rituals, potions, and chants to conjure up all sorts of trouble makes witchcraft mysterious and appealing.

These two areas of fantasy emerge on the screen as early as 1896. The films draw from literary sources, such as the writings of Dante and Milton or legends of Faust and Mephistopheles. Faust gave rise to many films, such as FAUST IN HELL (1897), DAMNATION OF FAUST, FAUST AND MARGUERITE, and DEVIL'S CASTLE (1896). Witch-oriented films never really gained notoriety, first appearing on the screen ten years later. MERRY FROLICS OF SATAN (1906), depicted an astral barouche led by skeletonlike steeds. DEVIL'S ASSISTANT (1918) was similar to A BARGAIN WITH SATAN

127

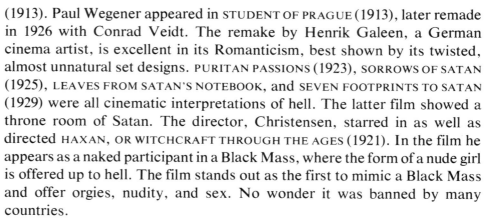

(1913). Paul Wegener appeared in STUDENT OF PRAGUE (1913), later remade in 1926 with Conrad Veidt. The remake by Henrik Galeen, a German cinema artist, is excellent in its Romanticism, best shown by its twisted, almost unnatural set designs. PURITAN PASSIONS (1923), SORROWS OF SATAN (1925), LEAVES FROM SATAN'S NOTEBOOK, and SEVEN FOOTPRINTS TO SATAN (1929) were all cinematic interpretations of hell. The latter film showed a throne room of Satan. The director, Christensen, starred in as well as directed HAXAN, OR WITCHCRAFT THROUGH THE AGES (1921). In the film he appears as a naked participant in a Black Mass, where the form of a nude girl is offered up to hell. The film stands out as the first to mimic a Black Mass and offer orgies, nudity, and sex. No wonder it was banned by many countries.

Dante inspired DANTE'S INFERNO (1935) with Spencer Tracy. The film was a remake of an earlier 1924 film. THE PRINCE OF TEMPTERS, THE DEVIL AND DANIEL WEBSTER, ALL THAT MONEY CAN BUY (1941), and ALIAS NICK BEAL (1947), all depicting the corruption of the human soul. The latter film showed corruption by the devil in politics. SEVENTH VICTIM (1943), was a Val Lewton film about a girl's struggle to free herself from the influence of a devil cult in Greenwich Village. Universal's THE BLACK CAT (1934) combines Boris Karloff and Bela Lugosi in a film on deviltry. Karloff is the leader of a devil cult who kills Lugosi's family while he is away. Upon discovering what happened during his absence, Lugosi enacts vengeance by skinning Karloff alive! I MARRIED A WITCH (1941), BEWITCHED, WOMAN WHO CAME BACK (1945), and WEIRD WOMAN (1944) all inspired the rise of the female as a source of evil in witch-oriented films. This film, based on Fritz Leiber's *Conjur Wife*, was remade in 1962 as BURN WITCH BURN, with Janet Blair as Tansy. She is a practicing witch who furthers her husband's career through black magic. The fifties brought FAUST AND THE DEVIL from Italy, BEAUTY AND THE DEVIL from France, and BLACK BUTTERFLIES from Mexico.

The best fifties film on the subject of demonology was Jacques Tourner's NIGHT OF THE DEMON (1958) for Columbia. Dana Andrews is John Holden, who investigates the mysterious death of a colleague. Neil McGinnes is Dr. Karswell, an evil conjuror who uses hurricanelike storms, balls of light, and panthers to bring destruction on those who challenge him. The appearance of a batlike demon that pursues Holden over the dark countryside is the film's best moment. The ultimate horror, saved until the

As long as fantasy films have been around, so have witches

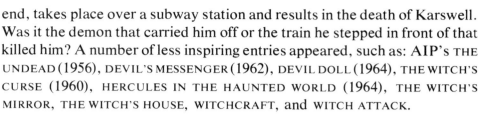

end, takes place over a subway station and results in the death of Karswell. Was it the demon that carried him off or the train he stepped in front of that killed him? A number of less inspiring entries appeared, such as: AIP's THE UNDEAD (1956), DEVIL'S MESSENGER (1962), DEVIL DOLL (1964), THE WITCH'S CURSE (1960), HERCULES IN THE HAUNTED WORLD (1964), THE WITCH'S MIRROR, THE WITCH'S HOUSE, WITCHCRAFT, and WITCH ATTACK.

The sixties brought an influx of witch-oriented films from many companies. The best film on the subject was Mario Bava's BLACK SUNDAY, made for AIP in 1961. The style of gloom conveyed by the use of ornate Gothic sets is captured by the rich black-and-white photography. The mood is unsurpassed in telling its tale of horror. Barbara Steele plays a witch who dies and is reborn to possess the soul of her descendent Katria, also played by Miss Steele. In the opening sequence the witch is condemned to death by her executioners in black hoods, who whip her. After this an iron mask is placed over her face and hammered into place, driving home spikes that pierce her skull! Barbara Steele went on to play another witch who possessed a newlywed bride in NMD's excellent SHE BEAST (1965). HORROR HOTEL (1963) was an effective horror tale in that the magical settings set up the evil to come. The mist-shrouded atmosphere of Whitewood, Massachusetts, with eerie people walking about in zombielike states, stages the first part of the film up to the sacrifice of the blonde student unwittingly sent there by her college professor. Nan Barlow (Venitia Stevenson) is executed in a Black Mass at the place where she has been doing her research on a witch who was condemned to the stake centuries ago by Pilgrims. THE DEVIL'S OWN (1967), HOUSE OF EVIL, EYE OF THE DEVIL, and Hammer's THE DEVIL RIDES OUT (1968), and THE DUNWICH HORROR (1969) all show how the devil exerts his influence over the good and pure through evil characters.

AIP's THE CONQUEROR WORM (1968) started a change in these films. The allegory of good and evil was shown graphically in a number of films in which witchfinders and clergy tortured their victims, who were consorts of the devil. Director Michael Reeves shows how sadism in the name of good purges the soul. Vincent Price plays Mathew Hopkins, a witchfinder general in the employ of Cromwellian England who goes about maiming and torturing suspect witches. Reeves shows how the common people's violence was inert and needed a catalyst like Hopkins to bring it out. Hopkins revels in the people's voyeuristic excitement in seeing his victims publicly

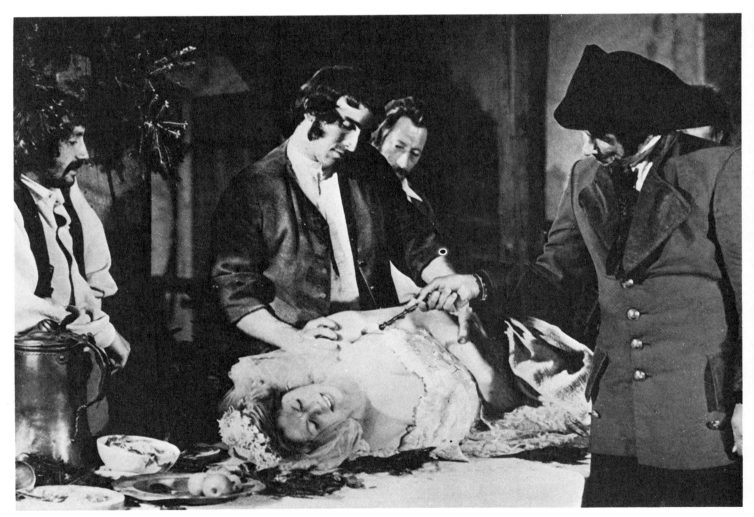

Torture for the sake of God and country in "Mark of the Devil"

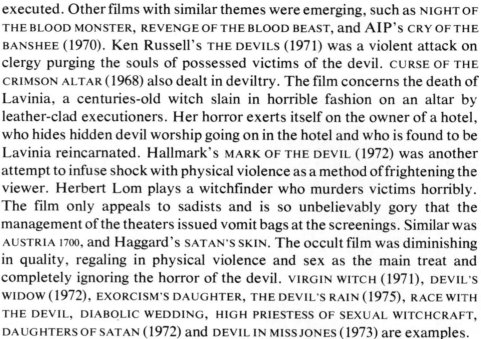

executed. Other films with similar themes were emerging, such as NIGHT OF THE BLOOD MONSTER, REVENGE OF THE BLOOD BEAST, and AIP's CRY OF THE BANSHEE (1970). Ken Russell's THE DEVILS (1971) was a violent attack on clergy purging the souls of possessed victims of the devil. CURSE OF THE CRIMSON ALTAR (1968) also dealt in deviltry. The film concerns the death of Lavinia, a centuries-old witch slain in horrible fashion on an altar by leather-clad executioners. Her horror exerts itself on the owner of a hotel, who hides hidden devil worship going on in the hotel and who is found to be Lavinia reincarnated. Hallmark's MARK OF THE DEVIL (1972) was another attempt to infuse shock with physical violence as a method of frightening the viewer. Herbert Lom plays a witchfinder who murders victims horribly. The film only appeals to sadists and is so unbelievably gory that the management of the theaters issued vomit bags at the screenings. Similar was AUSTRIA 1700, and Haggard's SATAN'S SKIN. The occult film was diminishing in quality, regaling in physical violence and sex as the main treat and completely ignoring the horror of the devil. VIRGIN WITCH (1971), DEVIL'S WIDOW (1972), EXORCISM'S DAUGHTER, THE DEVIL'S RAIN (1975), RACE WITH THE DEVIL, DIABOLIC WEDDING, HIGH PRIESTESS OF SEXUAL WITCHCRAFT, DAUGHTERS OF SATAN (1972) and DEVIL IN MISS JONES (1973) are examples.

ROSEMARY'S BABY (1969) was written and directed for the screen by Roman Polanksi from the best seller by Ira Levin. Producer Bill Castle is competent at evoking Gothic-style horror amidst the towers of glass and steel in Manhattan. The fact that we never see the child adds to the tension on the same principle of Val Lewton—that which we don't see but imagine is far more frightening. William Fredkin's Academy Award winner THE EXORCIST (1973) was based on William Peter Blatty's bestseller. The film deals with the demonic possession of a young girl, played by Linda Blair. The film's one basic flaw is that it never gets above the surface of its shock, using physical appearance to mark the girl's change from sweet Reagan to the evil, devilish girl. The room is cold, welts spell out "help" on her stomach, her eyes and tongue are like those of a snake; her head revolves in a complete circle. The film inspired a number of imitations that never approached THE EXORCIST in direction, screenplay, or special effects: ABBY (1974), BEYOND THE DOOR (1975), THEY CAME FROM WITHIN (1976), and PREMONITION. Twentieth Century Fox' THE OMEN (1976) shows how an antichrist or devil will come into the world amidst a sea of trouble and

The Druids resurrect their dying queen with fresh blood in
"Invasion of the Blood Farmers"

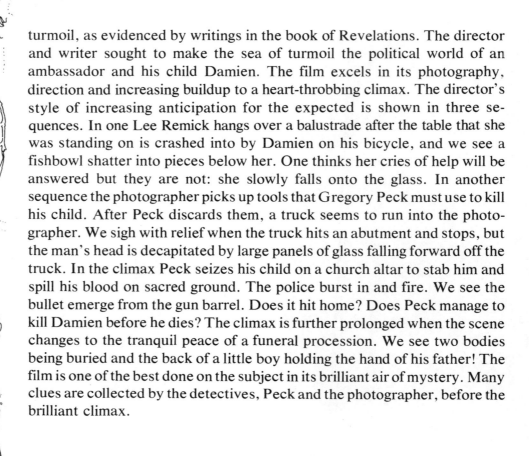

turmoil, as evidenced by writings in the book of Revelations. The director and writer sought to make the sea of turmoil the political world of an ambassador and his child Damien. The film excels in its photography, direction and increasing buildup to a heart-throbbing climax. The director's style of increasing anticipation for the expected is shown in three sequences. In one Lee Remick hangs over a balustrade after the table that she was standing on is crashed into by Damien on his bicycle, and we see a fishbowl shatter into pieces below her. One thinks her cries of help will be answered but they are not: she slowly falls onto the glass. In another sequence the photographer picks up tools that Gregory Peck must use to kill his child. After Peck discards them, a truck seems to run into the photographer. We sigh with relief when the truck hits an abutment and stops, but the man's head is decapitated by large panels of glass falling forward off the truck. In the climax Peck seizes his child on a church altar to stab him and spill his blood on sacred ground. The police burst in and fire. We see the bullet emerge from the gun barrel. Does it hit home? Does Peck manage to kill Damien before he dies? The climax is further prolonged when the scene changes to the tranquil peace of a funeral procession. We see two bodies being buried and the back of a little boy holding the hand of his father! The film is one of the best done on the subject in its brilliant air of mystery. Many clues are collected by the detectives, Peck and the photographer, before the brilliant climax.

"Blood on Satan's Claw"

chapter 13

FANTASY HEROES

AND HEROINES

A COMPLETE HISTORY of the fantasy film should include a look at the heroes that we grew up with and those with us today. The heroes emerged out of the pulps of the thirties and forties onto the screen. The antihero is comparable to his predecessors.

Edgar Rice Burroughs gave the literary world many tales of fantasy with his Tarzan of the jungles, David Innes of Pelucidar (the area beneath the earth's crust), and the chronicles of Carter on Mars. Tarzan became established as the first fantasy screen hero. He has been played by numerous actors, among them Lex Barker, Johnny Weismuller, and Ron Ely. TARZAN THE TIGER (1929) cast Frank Merrill, while Buster Crabbe donned the loincloth in TARZAN THE FEARLESS (1933). Two years later Herman Brix appeared in NEW ADVENTURES OF TARZAN. The character faced savage tribes, jungle animals, and even alien invaders from outer space! Tarzan's screen success continued into the early fifties.

Republic films gave Ralph Byrd the leading role in DICK TRACY, a 1936 serial based on Chester Gould's famous crime fighter. Byrd continued to portray Tracy in DICK TRACY RETURNS (1938), DICK TRACY VS CRIME INC. (1941), DICK TRACY'S G-MEN, and DICK TRACY MEETS DR. GRUESOME (1947). The evil Dr. Gruesome was portrayed by none other than Boris Karloff. Other comic heroes to enjoy screen popularity were: MANDRAKE THE MAGICIAN, played by Warren Hull for Columbia pictures; GREEN HORNET

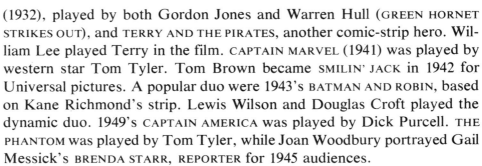

(1932), played by both Gordon Jones and Warren Hull (GREEN HORNET STRIKES OUT), and TERRY AND THE PIRATES, another comic-strip hero. William Lee played Terry in the film. CAPTAIN MARVEL (1941) was played by western star Tom Tyler. Tom Brown became SMILIN' JACK in 1942 for Universal pictures. A popular duo were 1943's BATMAN AND ROBIN, based on Kane Richmond's strip. Lewis Wilson and Douglas Croft played the dynamic duo. 1949's CAPTAIN AMERICA was played by Dick Purcell. THE PHANTOM was played by Tom Tyler, while Joan Woodbury portrayed Gail Messick's BRENDA STARR, REPORTER for 1945 audiences.

The most popular Fantasy hero of the thirties was Universal's FLASH GORDON, played by Buster Crabbe. The 1936 superbudgeted serial was based on Alex Raymond's comic strip. So successful was the film that it inspired two sequels, FLASH GORDON'S TRIP TO MARS and FLASH GORDON CONQUERS THE UNIVERSE (1940). The sequels never matched the quality of the original. The original's miniature special effects were well pieced together with the rest of the action, but the sequels suffered from poor positioning of the miniature shots and cuts to live action. Director Frederick Stephani's original had an aura of visual excitement, each episode ending in a cliff hanger. The sets were large and big-budgeted for a serial of its kind. The thirteen episodes became true classics. The film shows the planet Mongo on a collision course with Earth. Dr. Zarkov (Frank Shannon) and Dale Arden (Jean Rodgers) blast off with Flash in a rocket designed by Zarkov. After landing on Mongo the trio meet Ming the Merciless, played in grand red-herring style by Charles Middleton. Ming plans to conquer the Earth and sets Zarkov to work in his laboratory. Ming also has sexual designs on lovely blonde Dale, much to the disfavor of Flash. Flash is pitted against numerous fanged men, an orangopoid, and a gockyo, or lobsterlike monster, besides rescuing Dale from a fate worse than death (loss of virginity). He meets up with lethal sharkmen, Kala, and an octosac. Later the trio is captured by King Vulton and his Hawkmen. Joining forces with Thun and his Lionmen and Prince Baron, who was dethroned by Ming, the forces of good are victorious in saving the Earth from Ming's destruction. The films' excellence lies in Stefani's direction and screenplay, the special effects, and, most important, Frank Waxman's musical score.

The series, like most comics, pleased everyone with its non-stop action, impossible plots, gadgets and gimmicks, and the idea of the hero

Boris Karloff is a heroic blind sculptor in "Blind Man's Bluff"

engaging in action that we previously read about in the limited dimension of the comic strip. BUCK ROGERS (1939), also based on comic exploits and also starring Buster Crabbe, was another success. Buck is back with non-stop action and cliffhanging episodes. His exploits concern the domination of the world by a power-mad supercriminal, Killer Kane (Anthony Ward). Ward's style of sheer mayhem mimics the style of Ming. SUPERMAN and the sequel ATOM MAN VS SUPERMAN (1950), starred Kirk Alyn, but the hero became immensely popular on television as portrayed by George Reeves. Batman continued to retain popularity in the filmed version of the dynamic duo (1948), played by Robert Lowery and John Duncan. Americans weren't the only colorful heroes. Italy's heroes were strongarmed men from Greek and Roman myths. Among the screen heroes depicted were Hercules, Machiste, sons of Hercules, Ursus, Atlas, and Goliath, all played by good-looking big-bicep actors. Japanese heroes are more related to fantasy, except for the brief fad of the kung-fu movie. Starman and Octoman come from Japan. Run Run Shaw's company has brought to the cinema of the seventies Bruce Lee, Wang Yu, and Sonny Chiba as THE STREETFIGHTER. The violence is unbelievable as eyes are gouged out along with other vital organs. Mexico's heroes had one thing in common—unbelievable adventures with monsters, gangsters, and masked wrestlers. Mexico's heroes were all masked wrestlers, among them Santo, Blue Demon, and Wrestling Women.

The early sixties mingled tongue-in-cheek absurdity with science fiction, as seen in the James Bond thrillers based on Ian Fleming's super-sleuth Secret Agent 007. Bond is the typical antihero. The old hero was distinguished from the villain at first by white clothes in contrast to cloaks and hoods. The old hero didn't suffer from any vices and was shown as just a policeman bringing the criminal to justice, never issuing his own punishment but leaving that sort of thing to others. Capture meant restraint, not torture and physical violence. Bond is the contemporary Mike Hammer, carrying the role one further. While Hammer's style was based on realism, Bond mixed humor with elaborate technology. Bond was an unexcelled gambler and womanizer, well-educated in languages to wines. Bond saw fit to carry a license to kill. The James Bond films were popular because they bridge the gap between the plausible and the impossible in adult comic-strip films. They retain the slam-bang action and plots of the forties Saturday-afternoon-matinee hero while updating him.

"Flesh Gordon", the take-off on the tried and true "Flash Gordon"

DR. NO (1962) brought back the oriental villain in Joseph Weisman, out to destroy the U.S. missile program from an elaborate complex on an island, Crab Key. FROM RUSSIA WITH LOVE (1963) had 007 after a Russian decoder. The non-stop action and variety of gadgets were becoming an ever-increasing part of the film's popularity. Producers Harry Broccoli and Harry Saltzman went on to make GOLDFINGER (1964), about a madman's attempts to loot Fort Knox of its gold-bullion supply. THUNDERBALL (1965) took the action under the sea as 007 searched for two H-bombs to save the western powers from ransom by the evil forces of SPECTRE. The finale has a well-done underwater battle between good aquanauts and evil ones. YOU ONLY LIVE TWICE (1967) was the culmination of the sci-fi spy mixture. Here 007, played remarkably well by Sean Connery, is off to the Orient to search for the cause of space kidnappings of U.S. capsules. The elaborate set of a complex inside an inactive volcano, with a rocket launcher, gantry, pad, and other machinery, as a battleground between good and evil forces is breathtaking. The action of the Bond films is always highlighted by good music scores. John Barry can provide excellent action-oriented music. Sadly, this film was the last to employ an elaborate war between good and evil as a conclusion. DIAMONDS ARE FOREVER (1971), while it had a good plot about a laser station in a diamond-studded satellite that menaced the world, was Connery's last film. The film itself is more parody than anything. IN HER MAJESTY'S SECRET SERVICE (1969) substituted gimmicks and gadgets that were popular in the past for physical action atop a spa in the Swiss Alps. SPECTRE planned on biological warfare using lovely hypnotized girls from different countries. George Lazenby played Bond. Roger Moore picked up the role for United Artists in LIVE AND LET DIE (1973), about drugs and voodooism, and THE MAN WITH THE GOLDEN GUN (1974), with Christopher Lee as Francisco Scaramanga, a million-dollar hit man.

As the Bond hero became more associated with a fantasy-laden plot, he became more disassociated with the reality desired by the seventies audiences, who turned to the middle-class hero. Audiences identified with the hero who is visited upon by society's rapists, slayers, and sadists. Typical of the new wave of film heroes were Charles Bronson's DEATH WISH (1974) and Margeaux Hemmingway's LIPSTICK (1975). Bronson's family is raped and killed, which causes a passive character to take to the streets with a gun, blasting muggers and assorted sick characters. LIPSTICK tells of a model who is raped and enacts vengeance by blasting out his vitals with a high-powered rifle.

*"Goliath and the Vampires", an Italian import mixing mythology
with horror*